CRIMINOLOGY

SAGE FOCUS EDITIONS

CRIMINOLOGY
New Concerns

Edited by
EDWARD SAGARIN

Essays in Honor of Hans W. Mattick

 SAGE PUBLICATIONS   Beverly Hills   London

Portions of this volume appeared originally in the August 1978 (Volume 16, Number 2) issue of CRIMINOLOGY: *An Interdisciplinary Journal, the official publication of the American Society of Criminology.*

For information address:

SAGE PUBLICATIONS, INC.  SAGE PUBLICATIONS LTD
275 South Beverly Drive 28 Banner Street
Beverly Hills, California 90212 London EC1Y 8QE

Printed in the United States of America

Library of Congress Cataloging in Publication Data

Main entry under title:

Criminology, new concerns.

(Sage focus editions; 10)
Includes bibliographies.
CONTENTS: Sagarin, E. The concerns of criminologists.—
MacNamara, D. E. J. Hans W. Mattick, 1920-1978. —Jeffery, C. R.
Criminology as an interdisciplinary behavioral science. [etc.]
  1. Crime and criminals—Addresses, essays, lectures. 2. Crime
and criminals—United States—Addresses, essays, lectures.
3. Mattick, Hans W. 4. Mattick, Hans W.—Bibliography.
I. Mattick, Hans W. II. Sagarin, Edward, 1913-   III. Series.
HV6028.C78   364   79-14116
ISBN 0-8039-1275-7
ISBN 0-8039-1276-5 pbk.

FIRST PRINTING

CONTENTS

1

THE CONCERNS OF CRIMINOLOGISTS
A Foreword

Worldwide, the concerns of criminologists have risen, for few can any longer escape or explain away the rise in crime and the pervasive fear of crime that has become such an important part of everyday life. Crimes of governments against people and vice versa; kidnappings, both political and ordinary (meaning here nonpolitical, but having an irony of its own when it is realized that these acts are no longer extraordinary); white collar crime over which a few grow indignant; crime on the streets and in homes, in the poorest sections of the cities where the victims can least afford the losses and in suburbs and safe areas—these are but a few manifestations of the world around us.

The general public is concerned, for the most part as victims in the past or as potential victims; the politicians are of course concerned, as evidence of their failures or, in the case of the challengers, as clarion calls for a move to sweep out the old; police, legislators, and judges are concerned, their tasks made burdensome, sometimes dangerous, by the unfolding events. But what of criminologists?

Convinced as most of us are that something is new in crime, in the magnitude of the criminality, in the ubiquity of what has been called the victimity (a neologism for which there was a strong need), I sought to pose the question to a group of criminologists: What are your concerns in this period of high crime? Where can criminology turn? Do you have suggestions for some new focus, new theory, new area that requires attention? Do you see some answers on the horizon, some explanatory theories, some approaches that ought to be embraced?

Within the American Society of Criminology are to be found most of the leading criminologists in the United States, and quite a few from other points in the world. It was therefore decided, in bringing together this collection of original papers, to pose the question of the nature of their current concerns to a group of people all of whom are either former presidents of the American Society of Criminology or winners of one of the three scholarly awards usually presented annually (known as the Edwin Sutherland Award, for contributions in theory or research; the August Vollmer Award, for contributions in the administration of justice; and the Sellin-Glueck Award, in recognition of an outstanding scholar from abroad). Limited as we were in space, we were able to accommodate some 11 former presidents or awardees, half of whom chose to write with a colleague, an indication that some people (myself included) can find at least one other person with whom to agree, even in this era of fragmentation in the social sciences and sharp division within criminology.

We would be very pleased with the outcome if it were no more than 11 statements by people whose contributions in the field have made them worth listening to: Jeffery, Cressey, Wolfgang, Geis, and the others in the pages that follow. But out of this collection something more than the sum of all of the parts can be seen emerging. What appears here is some agreement that the answers so often offered in the past are no longer satisfactory; that a new situation does call for new directions on the part of criminology and criminologists; that old issues, as victimless crime and white-collar crime, are still with us but demand new approaches; and, finally, there is a leaning, almost a consensus, against being stampeded into the new hard-line orientation that could have been predicted as a concomitant of high crime rates.

The authors' works speak for themselves; they hardly need summary here, but perhaps a little interweaving, to delineate the relationships among them, might be helpful. The book starts with Jeffery, and while his central argument is focused on the need to move criminology into an interdisciplinary field, which for him means specifically seeing crime as a biosocial rather than a social product, he underlines past failures and warns against a new wave of ultrapunitive thinking. While the biosocial argument is not taken up by others in this series of articles (but it has many adherents, indeed), the call for new theory is echoed by many of the authors who follow, and the warning against capitulation to those punitively oriented is repeated. It will be found in Cressey, is stated most forthrightly by Glaser, is central to the argument of Sagarin and Karmen, and is troubling both Dinitz and Newman. Perhaps it should trouble all of us, for we do not have the answers, and having learned this, we have come a long way in criminology.

However, the sections of this book ought not exaggeratedly be thought of as all of a piece. They go off in the different directions that are rightly the concern of criminologists: theory, research, and policy. It is the research or, more specifically, problems of research, and specifically as applied to white collar crime, that demand the attention of the reader, and that is set forth by Clinard and Yeager. It is theory that ties together not only the orientations of Jeffery and Cressey, at least as set forth here, but of Wolfgang as well. And certainly all those who have written about punitive attitudes and repressive measures are explicitly dealing with policy. Nonetheless, Skolnick and Dombrink tackle a major issue in public policy: they address themselves to the question, "After decriminalization, what next?" There has been considerable discussion, and not a little legislative and judicial movement, toward decriminalization; and the works of Kadish on overcriminalization, of Schur on crimes without victims, of Geis on what he termed "not the law's business" have been not merely reflections of changing public sentiment but also contributions toward such change. Does decriminalization lead to institutionalization of formerly illegal behavior, to encouragement, or just what? We welcome this contribution toward what is still too meager a dialogue on such an important issue in criminology and public policy.

There is an interesting link between the articles by Wolfgang and by Geis and Meier, for both are looking backward and forward, Wolfgang in his own career in criminology and how his outlook has changed and Geis and Meier on the careers of people who were chosen, by a method outlined in their contribution, and how such people see their own concerns with criminology. But in a larger sense, that is what this book is all about: we are all looking backward, not nostalgically but with an effort for accurate reconstruction, and we are all trying to use this wisdom from hindsight when looking forward, so that the next generation will not have to bemoan our failures, and theirs.

This book, in short, is an effort at dialogue, not between a moderator and several others, not between two people or two points of view. But dialogue in which many people were asked to speak their minds and to speak on their concerns. We think more such dialogue is needed, not confined to criminology, of course, but criminology may need it more urgently than many other disciplines.

Hans Mattick spoke his mind, fearlessly and imaginatively, and in so doing made important contributions to our field. While this book was in preparation, Hans Mattick died, and we believe that it is a worthy tribute to him that we have dedicated our work to his memory.

—*Edward Sagarin*

New York
February 1979

2

HANS W. MATTICK
1920-1978

It was while a special issue of *Criminology: An Interdisciplinary Journal* was in preparation, an issue devoted to the concerns and anxieties that trouble criminologists in this period of apparently high crime rates, that I learned of the death of Hans Mattick. Here was a man whose entire adult life was one constant period of concern for the problems faced both by public and scholars, by victims and criminals, by wardens and prisoners. That issue of the journal, in a new and somewhat expanded form, is now presented as a book, and it seems not only fitting but indeed logical that the essays, in preparation at the time of the death of Hans Mattick, should be presented in his honor.

For nearly 30 years Hans Mattick was my friend, a friendship kept green more frequently by correspondence (letters, postcards, reprints, syllabi, reading lists) than by our all-too-infrequent get-togethers at conferences and on social occasions. We did not always agree, although on the major issues we were as one—capital punishment, penal reform, gun control, and the importance of practitioner experience for those who would teach criminology or criminal justice. We disagreed, sometimes rancorously, for Hans could defend his views almost as aggressively and as loudly as I, on the abolition of parole, on the use of police decoys, and on the necessity and value of abstract and theoretical contributions to criminological science.

Hans took his degrees at the University of Chicago, studying under Joseph Lohman, Lloyd Ohlin, Daniel Boorstin, and Albert Reiss, among others. Before joining the faculty, he served as a researcher for the RAND Corporation (1949-1950); was with the Illinois Parole and Pardon Board (1950-1955); was assistant warden of the Cook County Jail (1955-1958); supervisor of unemployment and compensation studies in the Office of the State Treasurer (1959-1960); and co-director of the Chicago Youth Development Project (1960-1965).

In 1966, Hans Mattick was named co-director with Norval Morris of the Center for Studies in Criminal Justice at the University of Chicago Law School; and in 1972 he was appointed Professor of Criminal Justice and Director of the Center for Research in Criminal Justice at the University of Illinois at Chicago Circle.

Hans Mattick served as president of the Illinois Academy of Criminology (1959-1960); as chairman of the Illinois Committee to Abolish Capital Punishment (1969-1978); as member of the Executive Council of the American Society of Criminology (1967-1971); as chairman of the Illinois Department of Corrections Advisory Board (1975-1976); as chairman of the Conference of Directors of Criminological Research Institutes (1967); and, among many other recognitions of his professional leadership in the field, as chairman of the Professional Advisory Committee of the John Howard League for Penal Reform (1957-1968). Among his many citations and commendations were the Governor's Justice Award; the Professional Achievement Award of the University of Chicago Alumni Association; the Annual Award of the John Howard Association; and scrolls from the Criminal Justice Commission of Chicago-Cook County, the Illinois Academy of Criminology, and the American League to Abolish Capital Punishment.

Hans Mattick and I shared a "boss," Donald H. Riddle, who, after a decade as president of the John Jay College of Criminal Justice, was named chancellor of the University of Illinois at Chicago Circle. I can do no better than quote a few lines from the eulogy Donald Riddle gave at the memorial tribute in Bond Chapel of the University of Chicago, on February 28, 1978:

> Hans was the ideal practitioner-scholar. . . . [He] used the knowledge and insights of the one to inform and temper the performance in the other. . . . The range of his mind inspired awe. Officially a social scientist, in fact in the deeper recesses of his heart and soul he was a humanist and he never accepted the constraints imposed by the artificial compartmentalization of knowledge of the academic world. . . . His mind was like his office, piled high with what appeared to be clutter, but in reality filed and ordered for ready access. . . . He understood, in his mind but even more deeply in his heart, the human condition; and shared both the despair and hope to which that understanding gives rise. . . . He often hated what people did and always hated some of the things people *could* do, but he was always sensitive to the common bonds of humanity, to the wellsprings of human behavior, and to the fine line between good and evil. By example he made one almost believe in rehabilitation, if only there were enough Hans Matticks to go around.

The Chicago *Tribune*, in an editorial published on January 28, 1978, entitled "Hans Mattick—The Limitless Man," depicted him faithfully:

> Hans Mattick was a big, burly bear of a man with a gravelly voice and a heart huge enough to care for all the cripples of our complicated society: people who suffered from crime and people who committed crime; kids tortured and abused by their parents and parents so tortured they abused their kids; bad schools, bad prisons, slums which grow worse no matter how many urban improvement projects are launched. He cared and fought with limitless energy and optimism. At least, he made us think it was limitless.

Hans Mattick was a native of Germany. My command of his native tongue is weak. But in Irish we say of one such as Hans Mattick: Ar dheis De go raibh a anam dilis. Ni bheidh a leitheid aris ann. [May he sit on the right hand of God. You will not see his like again.]

Hans Mattick: May this volume be a modest expression of the high esteem in which you were held by those of us who had the good fortune to know you.

Requiescat in Pace.

Donal E. J. MacNamara
John Jay College of Criminal Justice

Hans W. Mattick: A Selected Bibliography

Between 1945 and 1977, Hans Mattick published more than 90 books, articles, and reports. A few of the most important publications, presented chronologically, are given below.

1959   Some latent functions of imprisonment. Journal of Criminology, Criminal Law and Police Science, Vol. 50, No. 3.

1960   Parolees in the army during World War II. Federal Probation, Vol. 24, No. 3.

1963   The Unexamined Death. Chicago: John Howard Association.

1964   The Chicago Youth Development Project. Ann Arbor: Institute for Social Research, University of Michigan.

1964   Factors affecting the process and outcome of street club work. Sociology and Social Research, Vol. 48, No. 2.

1966   The epidemiology of drug addiction and reflections on the problem and policy in the United States. Illinois Medical Journal, Vol. 130, No. 4.

1967   The future of imprisonment in a free society. British Journal of Criminology, Vol. 7, No. 4.

1968   The form and content of recent riots. University of Chicago Law Review, Vol. 35, No. 4.

1969   The cloacal region of American corrections. The Annals of the American Academy of Political and Social Science, Vol. 381.

1969   Action on the Streets. New York: Association Press.

1970   Illinois Jails: Challenge and Opportunity for the 1970s. Chicago: Illinois Law Enforcement Council.

1972   The Prosaic Sources of Prison Violence. Occasional Papers, University of Chicago Law School.

1973   The pessimistic hypothesis and an immodest proposal. Public Welfare, Vol. 31, No. 2.

1974   The contemporary jails of the United States. In Daniel Glaser, ed., Handbook of Criminology. Chicago: Rand McNally.

1975   Reflections of a former prison warden. In James Short, ed., On Delinquency, Crime and Society. Chicago: University of Chicago Press.

3

CRIMINOLOGY AS AN
INTERDISCIPLINARY BEHAVIORAL SCIENCE

C. R. JEFFERY
Florida State University

While I was a graduate student at Indiana University (1947-1951) I came into contact with Edwin Sutherland, who presented a sociological version of crime causation. He was total in his rejection of biology and psychology, following the maxim from Durkheim that social behavior must be explained at the social level. This position has dominated sociological criminology and has limited explanations of criminal behavior to social variables.

While at Indiana I came across an article by Jerome Hall, a legal philosopher and distinguished professor of jurisprudence and criminal law at Indiana. In his article, Hall argued that criminologists did not understand crime since they were totally devoted to the positivistic school of criminology or, as he said, were "whole-hog positivistic." Hall's contrast of the positivist school and the classical school of criminology so intrigued me that I wrote my disseration on the topic of the origins of crime within the social and legal structure, an approach now referred to as labeling theory and conflict criminology. I found it hard to understand how American criminologists could be so limited in the assumptions they made about crime and criminals (Jeffery, 1956).

Also while at Indiana I heard about a strange man who was saying a science of behavior was possible if we would give up our introspective and mentalistic views of behavior. B. F.

Skinner was a radical learning theorist who was still struggling at that time to have his notions of operant conditioning accepted in psychology. Graduate students in sociology did not discuss behaviorism because symbolic interactionism was the dogma of the day. Sometimes over a beer we would whisper such dirty words as conditioning, behavior, and reinforcement. Later on, while at Arizona State, the "Fort Skinner of the West," I became a behaviorist, as seen in my work in learning theory and criminal behavior (Jeffery, 1965, 1977).

While still a graduate student, I asked myself how it was possible to have three giants such as Sutherland, Hall, and Skinner within 100 yards of each other without any significant mutual interaction. They might as well have been on different planets, so far as graduate education in criminology was concerned at Indiana. Whatever benefit I gained from the three came from my own personal sacrifice and effort.

In recalling my own experiences with criminology within the context of law, sociology, psychology, and biology, I can only conclude that criminology must be an interdisciplinary behavioral science. If, as Sutherland argued, criminology involves the making of laws, the breaking of laws, and the reaction to the breaking of laws, then all criminological propositions are propositions concerning *behavior.* Behavior is what we study as criminologists. We cannot understand law or deviance from law or the social reaction to norm violations without first having a *basic theory of behavior.* If, as Sutherland argued, behavior is *learned,* then we must concentrate our attention in criminology on learning theory as found in biology and psychology, and thus bring Sutherland and criminology into the twentieth century.

Two major problems emerge immediately if we are to regard criminology as a behavioral science. (1) Criminology does not have a theory of behavior, and, in fact, does not even focus its attention on either criminal behavior or behavior. (2) Criminology is confused with criminal justice and the eighteenth-century legal view of man, deterrence, retribution, and justice. Criminal justice means the police, courts, and prisons. It is assumed that this is the correct and only way in which the crime problem can be conceived. We in criminology are so dominated by the legal and political issues involved in law enforcement, court administration, and prison administration that we have a difficult time defining criminology. Politicians say we need more police, not more professors, and we encourage our professors to become police.

Criminology is dominated by the nineteenth-century view of the psychosocial nature of man. Criminal justice is dominated by the eighteenth-century view of political man. The assumptions we make about human nature must be challenged.

BASIC ASSUMPTIONS OF CLASSICAL CRIMINOLOGY

The following statements represent the classical approach to crime control.

1. Crime is a legal process. This is a *justice* model of crime control, involving both a *crime control* model of the police and a *due process* model of the lawyer (Packer, 1968).

2. The major weapon against crime is *punishment*. Punishment acts as a deterrent to those who commit crimes and to those who are about to commit crimes, and it acts as a source of retribution and revenge for those who do the punishing (Newman, 1978).

3. If we put people in institutions (Rothman, 1971), we will handle the crime problem. We can make better citizens out of criminals (most of whom come from brutal and neglecting environments) by subjecting them to the brutalization of our prisons.

4. We can control crime by waiting until the crime occurs and then taking action. In this way we can insure a large "crimes unknown to police" figure, a small "arrest by police" figure, a large "plea bargaining" figure, and a small "sent to prison" figure. We can also insure a large "number of victims" figure and a high "cost of crime" figure.

5. We can control crime by leaving the environment in which crimes occur untouched.

6. We can control crime by leaving the personality structure of the criminal untouched.

7. Criminals are not to be treated. Criminal law is for those who voluntarily and immorally violate the law. They deserve punishment. We can only treat those whose behavior has been caused by a mental disease. If a man is insane he is treated; if he is guilty he is punished (Jeffery, 1967).

8. We have no legal guarantees for the treatment of those who are accused of crimes. All we have is due process for the punishment of those found guilty of crime (Kittrie, 1971).

9. We know all we need to know about human behavior to operate the criminal justice system. The criminal justice system and crime control policy must be in the hands of politicians, police, lawyers, and prison guards. Biologists, psychologists, and sociologists are not allowed to testify as to the causes of criminal behavior, nor does federal policy encourage basic research on criminal behavior.

BASIC ASSUMPTIONS OF POSITIVISTIC CRIMINOLOGY

1. Crime can be cured by treatment. Punishment of the offense must be replaced with treatment of the offender. Individual differences must be taken into account in sentencing and disposition of criminals.

2. We need not be concerned about the legal and ethical aspects of a treatment model.

3. We need not be concerned about the lack of a basic theory of behavior in psychology or sociology which will allow us to treat criminal behavior successfully.

4. We need not change the environment in which crimes occur in order to reduce the crime rate.

5. We need not change criminal behavior in order to change the criminal. We can change his mind with its internal conflicts (psychoanalysis), or we change his education, job train-

ing, opportunity structure, or socioeconomic status (sociology).

6. We can develop biological, psychological, and sociological theories of behavior in total isolation from one another and still have a sound basis for criminological theory.

7. The proper time to treat the criminal is after he is mature and vicious. We need not worry about prevention techniques which would start at the prenatal period.

THE FAILURES OF CRIMINOLOGY AND CRIMINAL JUSTICE

As Radzinowicz (1977) reminds us, the failures of criminology and criminal justice are found in such facts as (a) we have more people in custody in the United States than any other country reporting, (b) we have more people in custody than at any time in history, (c) we are experiencing a 60%-70% recidivism rate, (d) we have no evidence that punishment and deterrence are solutions to the crime problem, and (e) we have no theory of behavior in criminology that stands close scrutiny.

The growth of a psychological model of treatment à la Freud resulted in the failure of psychology and psychiatry to help the crime problem (Lewis and Balla, 1976). At the same time, there were many violations of the legal rights of those supposedly in treatment (Kittrie, 1971). The merger of law and psychiatry created such tragic programs as exemplified by the Patuxent Institution. When Patuxent was closed in 1976, many criminologists regarded it as the end of a bold experiment in the use of psychology as a rehabilitative tool (American Academy, 1977).

The failure of psychiatry and psychology during the 1920-1950 era is matched by the failure of the sociological model as found in the war against poverty program in the 1960 era. The notion that the opportunity structure could be altered through education and job training, thus altering poverty and delinquency, was also a total disaster (Jeffery, 1977; Radzinowicz, 1977). The failure of criminology as a science of the individual offender was matched by its failure as a science of the social offender.

In 1933 Michael and Adler (1933) reminded us that criminology was a failure, a viewpoint restated later by Lady Wootton (1959; see also Mueller, 1969). In 1967 the President's Commission noted that until a science of behavior matures beyond its present confines, an understanding of delinquency is not likely to be forthcoming. Out of this emerged the Safe Streets Act and the Law Enforcement Assistance Administration.

The failure of LEAA to meet the challenge of crime is by now well documented (Serrill, 1976b). According to the National Academy of Sciences Report (White and Krislov, 1977), NILECJ assumed that a body of knowledge existed and all that was necessary was to apply it. Crime control was viewed not as a problem in criminology and behavioral science, but as a problem for law enforcement, courts, and prisons. In other words, criminal justice would solve our problems, not criminology. LEAA made an attempt to pour money into technology and hardware for the police in an effort to reduce the crime rate, and when this failed it shifted from crime control to improving the operation of the criminal justice system. According to the NAS report, the Institute "avoided the hard questions of knowledge about crime and criminal behavior in favor of the easier but relatively trivial studies of systems operations." The NAS report recommends a commitment to basic research in the behavioral sciences to be done by professionals and not practitioners. Such a program would be devoted to the accumulation of scientific knowledge rather than training, service programs, or technical assistance.

In a memorandum to President Carter, Attorney General Bell (1977) noted that LEAA was a paper-shuffling operation which had failed to come up with new and innovative means to combat the ever-growing crime problem.

A U.N. report (1977) based on a worldwide survey found that the traditional methods developed over the ages to deal with crime have not proven successful, and in some instances have aggravated the situation. The U.N. report concluded that we must identify the factors involved in criminality before we can make policy for its control.

The failure of the criminal justice system has led to such movements as community-based corrections, diversionary programs, deinstitutionalization, decriminalization, and a plea that doing nothing is better than doing something. Such diversionary and avoidance tactics, however, often result in "alternative encapsulation" in another system, usually without benefit of due process of law (Klein et al., 1976). Sarri and Vinter (1976), from their National Assessment of Juvenile Corrections project, conclude that the juvenile justice system is grossly overloaded, ineffective, and indifferent to basic human rights. They note that we are involved in decriminalization, diversion, deinstitutionalization, deterrence, punishment, and retribution, all in the same program. They conclude that "failures are easily found, but what seems particularly disturbing today is the lack of learning from past experience by key decision makers."

The failure of the treatment model in criminology—that is, the failure of criminology—led to the LEAA program of the 1970s with an emphasis on law and order, punishment, and bigger and better prisons. We are told we cannot know the causes of criminal behavior. We are told we cannot prevent crime. This is the Martinson "nothing works" era. The experts of the 1970s, such as Wilson, Morris, Fogel, and Von Hirsch, are advocating a return to punishment and prisons, to the use of fixed sentences, to sentences based on the crime and not the criminal. This philosophy does not allow for discretion, and it depends on larger police departments and more prisons to solve the crime problem (Jeffery, 1977; Serrill, 1976a). Involuntary treatment is not allowed, but we do allow the execution of criminals or their confinement to snake pits for life. In the 1970s the legal view that man cannot be treated but must be punished comes once again into full bloom.

We have given up the treatment model at a time when the behavioral sciences are about to make a major contribution to our knowledge of human behavior. It is ironic that in the 1970s, when we are returning to an eighteenth-century punishment model of crime control, twenty-first-century breakthroughs are occurring in our understanding of human behavior.

FAILURES OF PAST THEORIES OF BEHAVIOR

In the past, psychology and sociology have made certain assumptions about human behavior which have limited our ability to understand behavior and to apply such knowledge to the treatment of mental illness and crime.

1. Inferences are made about internal micro-aspects of behavior. It is recognized that once a stimulus enters the organism, something happens to it before it influences behavior, but what happens is never known. Man is viewed as possessing reason, volition, and emotion, but these processes are never subject to direct observation. A "black box" is created wherein a stimulus goes in and a response comes out. In order to explain what comes out we resort to the concept of a mind or mental processes which cause behavior. The method for studying the mind is *introspection*. From introspection we derive explanatory concepts for behavior, usually labeled attitudes, self-concepts, or perceptions of the environment.

2. Related to the above is that direct observations of behavior are seldom if ever made. Indirect observations are the norms, as found in psychiatric therapies, verbal reports, test scores, attitude questionnaires, and the like. The usual method of study is to ask the subject a question and then rely on his test score or verbal report. As Nettler (1978) has noted, asking people questions about their behavior is a poor way of observing it.

In criminology this is especially critical, for as criminologists we seldom study behavior. What we study are records of behavior, or test scores from prisoners, or verbal reports from prisoners. Ask yourself sometime to list the number of studies you know of which make direct observations of criminal behavior.

3. The theory of *equipotentiality* dominates a great deal of psychological and sociological thought. This doctrine denies genetic differences and holds that each individual possesses the same potentiality for learning behavior in a given environment. This is another way of stating the doctrine of *environmentalism*, that is, behavior is a product of environmental influences.

4. Not only is the environment the supreme determinant of behavior, but it is the *social* environment and not the *physical* environment.

5. There is a separation of biology, psychology, and sociology into separate disciplines. An integrated theory of behavior as advocated by systems theory (Kuhn, 1975; Klir, 1972) must be developed.

The sociological position follows this model of behavioral analysis. Behavior is caused by a desire to conform to norms or to the expectations of others. The major explanation in sociology is the internalization of norms (Scott, 1971). Peple behave as they do because of norms, attitudes, values, and beliefs. As Hirschi (1969) noted, there are no explanations of deviance in this approach, only explanations of conformity. Sociologists come up with two explanations of deviance out of conformity. Either the normative system is blocked, as in anomie theory, or the norms are in conflict, as in cultural conflict and differential association theory.

Sociologists deal with age, sex, ethnic background, and urban areas as major correlates of crime rates. These are viewed as social variables, whereas a little reflection will reveal that they are biological and social variables. There is no such thing as a social variable; there are only biosocial variables.

Behaviorism as found in Pavlov, Watson, and Skinner overcame the methodological problems found in introspective psychology; that is, behaviorism moved to the direct observation of behavior, but behaviorism ignored the genetic and brain variables involved in learning (Jeffery, 1977). The behaviorist observed the stimulus and the response without anything connecting the two. Thus behaviorism perpetuated the principles of *equipotentiality* and *environmentalism*. Even the Russians with Lysenko have not been more complete in their doctrine of environmental determinism. Behaviorism has had a very small impact on sociology or criminology, and my attempt to move criminology from Sutherland to Skinner was met in criminology with a return to Sutherland and social reinforcement theory (Jeffery, 1977).

The impact of behaviorism on institutional practices, as found in behavioral therapies, token economies, and managed contingencies projects, has been enormous. The results have been disappointing (Jeffery, 1977).

A NEW MODEL: BIOSOCIAL CRIMINOLOGY

ELEMENTS OF THE NEW MODEL

The new model must contain several basic elements now absent in criminology: (1) It must move from deterrence, punishment, and treatment to *prevention*. (2) It must move from a social to a *physical environment*. (3) It must move from a social to a *biosocial* model of learning.

Crime Prevention

By crime prevention we mean those actions taken before a crime is committed to reduce or eliminate the crime rate. The public health model of medical care is a prevention model. Today medicine is more concerned with the prevention of heart disease and cancer than with the treatment and institutional-ization of those already afflicted.

The present criminal justice model waits for the crime to occur before responding. The LEAA and federal government response has been to increase the capacity of the criminal justice system. The more police we have, the more arrests; the more arrests, the more courts and lawyers; the more courts, the more prisons; the more prisons, the more people who will return to prisons.

Behavior is the product of two sets of variables: a *physical environment* and a *physical organism* in interaction. Crime prevention must be based on a social ecology which recognizes the interaction of man and environment as complementary physical systems in interactions.

On January 3, 1978, there was a special on medicine in America on NBC news. In this program the Delta Health Center in Mississippi was discussed in detail. The Delta project was established by a community health group at Tufts University to prevent disease among the rural poor of the Delta. They were concerned with such variables as diet, sanitary conditions, food supplies, inoculations, preventive physical care, and preventive medicine in general. The disease rate dropped immediately, and the clinics and hospitals for the sick were almost empty. Then Washington and the federal government decided that monies would not be available for disease control, but only for the treatment of those already diseased. Payments were made for X rays, surgery, medications, hospital costs, and other expenses connected with being ill. Within a few months the hospitals in the Delta were again filled with sick people, with people standing in long lines all day long in hope of getting some medical care.

The more hospitals and mental institutions we build, the more sick people we have. The more prisons and courts we build, the more criminals we have. We have made the "Delta Plan" national policy.

The Physical Environment

Criminology must move from Sutherland, Shaw, and McKay, from the cultural conflict perspective, to a physical environment perspective (Jeffery, 1976). Crime rates are highly correlated with the physical features of the environment, such as buildings, streets, parks, automobiles, and highways. Most areas of the urban environment are crime-free; crime is very selective in where it occurs. Some blocks have many murders and robberies, others have none. Crime prevention involves the design of physical space. This is a joining of urban design, environmental psychology, and social ecology into a meaningful relationship.

Last year I was in a gymnasium on the Florida State campus to watch a dance review, and my daughter had to use the bathroom facilities which were located in the basement. At that time I remarked how this was a perfect environment for a mugging and/or rape. Within a month a rape occurred there, one of many on the campus. On January 15, 1978 two coeds were murdered and three brutally attacked on the campus. The intruder gained entrance to a sorority house by means of an unlocked door. The police are now spending thousands of dollars and thousands of man-hours on the case, the politicians want to execute the bastard, and yet this predictable response has not helped the dead girls or their families and friends, nor has it reduced the level of hysteria and fear on this campus. As I am writing this article, there is another radio account of an attempted rape on campus over the past weekend.

Biosocial Criminology

The new criminology must represent a merging of biology, psychology, and sociology. It must reflect the hierarchies of sciences as found in systems analysis (Figure 1).

Behavior reflects both genetic and environmental variables. The equipotentiality environmentalism of the past must be

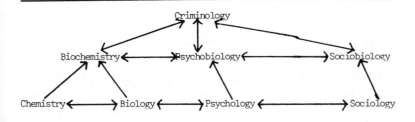

Figure 1

replaced with a model which clearly recognizes that each and every individual is different genetically (except perhaps for MZ twins). Williams (1967), a biochemist and past president of the American Chemical Society, argues that only 15% of the population has what is termed normal anatomical features. If our noses varied as much as our hearts and kidneys and hormonal systems, some of us would have noses the size of beans, others would have noses the size of watermelons.

The sociologist/criminologist often assumes that if behavior is learned, then learning in no way involves biology or psychology. This argument ignores the fact that learning is a psychobiological process involving changes in the biochemistry and cell structure of the brain. Learning can only occur if there are physical changes in the brain. The process is best summarized as a system of information flow from environment to organism:

$$\frac{\text{Genetic}}{\text{code}} \times \text{Environment} = \frac{\text{Brain}}{\text{code}} \times \text{Environment} = \text{BEHAVIOR}$$

Genetic codes and brain codes are of a biochemical nature, involving the biochemical structure of genes and of neutral transmission in the brain. The type of behavior (response) exhibited by an organism depends on the nature of the environment (stimulus) and the way in which the stimulus is coded, transmitted, and decoded by the brain and nervous system.

This is what is meant by the biological limitations on learning (Jeffery, 1977).

We do not inherit behavior any more than we inherit height or intelligence. We do inherit a capacity for interaction with the environment. Sociopathy and alcoholism are not inherited, but a biochemical preparedness for such behaviors are present in the brain which, if given a certain type of environment, will produce sociopathy or alcoholism.

The brain contains a center for emotion and motivation, based on pleasure and pain, a center for reason and thought, and a center for the processing of information from the environment. This is almost a Freudian model put within the context of modern psychobiology, as suggested by Pribram and Gill (1976) in their work on the new Freud. The concept of social control is a neglected theory in criminology, although it is to be found in Reckless, Nye, Hirschi, and others. Certainly biosocial learning theory, as I have presented it, is control theory. In summary, what biosocial control theory holds is that behavior is controlled by the brain. Behavior involves biochemical changes in the neurons which then activate muscles and glands. An incoming impulse or experience from the social environment must be encoded, stored, acted upon, and decoded by the brain before it comes out as social behavior. Social behavior, be it conforming or deviant, must go into a brain and come out of a brain. G. H. Mead made this a basic part of his social behaviorism, but this has been totally neglected by the symbolic interactionists.

EMERGING ISSUES IN CRIMINOLOGY

If one regards behavior as a product of the interaction of a physical organism with a physical environment, then one must be prepared to find different sorts of things in criminology in the near future, assuming the courage to look for them. Gordon (1976) and Hirschi and Hindelang (1977) have in recent articles suggested a link between low intelligence and delinquency. Mednick and his associates found that 41.7% of the XYY cases identified in Denmark had a history of criminal careers, compared to 9% of the XY population. They also found that the link between XYY and criminality was not aggression and high testosterone levels but rather low intelligence. They also found that criminals from the XY population had low intelligence. Since genes interact with one another, this suggests the possibility that the Y chromosome is involved in those biochemical processes labeled intelligence (Mednick and Christiansen, 1977).

Intelligence is related to both genetics and environment (Oliverio, 1977; Halsey, 1977; Stine, 1977). This means the impact of poverty and social class on crime rates must be reinterpreted in terms of intelligence. Education and social class are influenced by intelligence, as well as influencing intelligence. To take one example, protein intake is a crucial variable in brain development and thus intelligence. Protein intake is also very dependent on the educational and socio-economic background of the parents. The link between poverty and crime is intelligence and protein intake, at least as one of several interacting variables.

Criminal and delinquent behaviors have also been related to learning disabilities, hypoglycemia, epilepsy, perceptual difficulties, and sociopathy (Hippchen, 1978; Lewis and Balla, 1976; Williams and Kalita, 1977).

The new model of treatment emerging in biological psychiatry is one involving the biochemistry of the brain (Rosenthal and Kety, 1968; Brady et al., 1977; Maser and Seligman, 1977; Van Praag and Bruinvels, 1977; Hamburg and Brodie, 1975). The genetic factor in mental disorders in now well recognized. Dopamine and norepinephrine levels in the brain are related to behavioral disorders; the more norepinephrine, the greater the level of excitation, as in schizophrenia; the lower the norepinephrine level, the lower the level of excitation, as in sociopathy and depression.

The use of drugs in the treatment of behavioral disorders has resulted in a dramatic decrease in institutionalization for schizophrenics. Chlorpromazine (thorazine) is the major drug used in the United States (Julien, 1975). Lithium to treat depression has received widespread publicity because of its use in the case of Tony Orlando, the popular television star. Lithium and thorazine act to block the norepinephrine post-synaptic sites, thus reducing the amount of norepinephrine available for the neurochemical transmission of information. As noted, behavior depends on the encoding and decoding of information by the brain.

A PRIVATE CRIMINAL JUSTICE SYSTEM

The future of crime control must depend on the development of a crime prevention program involving both the physical organism and the physical environment. The environmental design aspects of crime control must be addressed within the structure of federal policy concerning housing and urban design. The more crucial issue, as far as implementation of policy is concerned, is at the level of the individual offender.

In order to implement a biosocial approach to crime prevention, we must have early diagnosis and treatment of neurological disorders. This will mean experimentation and research. It will mean brain scans and blood tests. It will mean tests for learning disabilities and hypoglycemia. All of this involves medical examinations, intrusions into the privacy of the individual, and controversial and experimental surgeries and/or drug therapies. Under such circumstances, and with as much opposition as exists today to the control of human behavior by the state system, it will be difficult if not impossible to turn biomedical research over to a federal agency.

Because of the major failures of the federal government with health, education, and welfare problems, including crime, and because of the great dangers attendant upon the use of behavioral control systems by the state, it is recommended that a private treatment system be set up to parallel or to replace the present criminal justice system. The treatment of behavioral disorders, including those labeled as crime, must be removed *from the political arena.* The lawyer and politician are so committed to a given view of human nature and justice that an impossible gap has been created between the behavioral sciences and the criminal justice system. The administration of LEAA in the Department of Justice is a beautiful example of what happens to crime control policy in the political arena.

A private treatment system would be established at two or three major research centers, hopefully associated with major medical research centers. At such a clinic a complete medical and behavioral history would be taken, including a complete neurological work-up as described by Lewis in her book on the New Haven clinic. Treatment would flow from a total assessment of the behavioral state of the individual. Such services would be on a voluntary basis, as it is for cancer, kidney disorders, and heart disease.

Since such clinics would be expensive, private funds must be sought. A new policy must be established wherein public funds could be transferred to such clinics if they accept cases from the current criminal justice system. The state would save a great deal of money by transferring cases to the private sector. This would be established as a part of the existing legal doctrine of "right to treatment." Under such a doctrine no one would be denied needed medical care, including medical attention for brain disorders. Mental illness has been redefined as physical illness by biological psychiatry, and it should have the same legal status as a heart attack or cancer of the colon. We worry about not providing counsel for a defendant before we send him to the electric chair or to prison, but we do not show the same amount of concern for placing neurologically disordered people in prison. We worry about the insanity defense and all the nonsense it has produced about behavioral disorders, but we do not ask why the definitions of insanity do not include those found today in biological psychiatry. We would rather put Charles Manson in prison or put Gary Gilmore before a firing squad than spend the time and money needed to find out why they became what they became.

It has been proposed for years that a voucher system be created by the state for its educational system. Such a system would allow students to select the elementary or high schools they want to attend, and they would then buy their education. In this way the school becomes directly responsible to the client. In the same way I propose a voucher system for criminal justice.

Each defendant could spend his voucher where he wanted. If he was not helped by the clinic, then the clinic would have failed him. Unsuccessful treatments would be driven out of existence once we make those engaged in treatment responsible for the outcome of the treatment.

It goes without saying that a major research effort is needed to join biology, medicine, psychology, criminology, and criminal law into a new crime prevention model. We must approach the crime problem as a behavioral problem and not as a political problem. We must recognize that the police, courts, and corrections cannot handle a genetic defect, hypoglycemia, or learning disabilities any more than they can handle cancer or heart disease.

We continue to pour millions into the criminal justice system under the illusion that the police, courts, and prisons are the answer to the crime problem. We continue to rely on lawyers and politicians, not behavioral scientists. We continue to ignore criminology and the behavioral sciences. An $825 million investment in several major research centers over the next few years would have a major impact on our ability to understand behavior. This money given to thousands of local police departments will have a negative effect. The more police we have, the more courts we have, the more prisons we have, the more criminals we have. Again, Washington has failed to learn from its past failures.

I realize that this paper is caught in the winds of an era powered by fixed sentencing and punishment with justice. The denial of the rehabilitative and medical model for criminology is such today that my plea for a behavioral criminology is unlikely to receive a very warm reception. However, this is nothing new with me, and I have patience and faith in history and in the human animal.

For those who insist on being on the stormy water of criminology, as I do, I offer the following:

A Ship in Harbor is Safe
But That is Not What
A Ship is Made For

REFERENCES

American Academy of Psychiatry and the Law (1977) "Patuxent Institution." Bulletin 5: 116-271.

BELL, G. (1977) "Memorandum for the president: the Law Enforcement Assistance Administration." November 21.

BRADY, J. P. (1977) Psychiatry. New York: Spectrum.

GORDON, R. (1976) "Prevalence: the rare datum in delinquency," in M. Klein (ed.) The Juvenile Justice System. Beverly Hills, CA: Sage.

HALSEY, A. H. (1977) Heredity and Environment. New York: Free Press.

HAMBURG, D. and H. BRODIE (1975) American Handbook of Psychiatry, Vol. 6: New Psychiatric Frontiers. New York: Basic Books.

HIPPCHEN, L. (1978) The Ecologic-Biochemical Approaches to Treatment of Delinquents and Criminals. New York: Van Nostrand Reinhold.

HIRSCHI, T. (1969) The Causes of Delinquency. Berkeley: Univ. of California Press.

——— and M. HINDELANG (1977) "Intelligence and delinquency." Amer. Soc. Rev. 42: 571-586.

JEFFERY, C. R. (1977) Crime Prevention Through Environmental Design. Beverly Hills, CA: Sage.

—— (1976) "Criminal behavior and the physical environment." Amer. Behav. Scientist 20: 149-174.

—— (1967) Criminal Responsibility and Mental Disease. Springfield, IL: Thomas.

—— (1965) "Criminal behavior and learning theory." J. of Criminal Law, Criminology, and Police Sci. 56: 294-300.

—— (1956) "The structure of American criminological thinking." J. of Criminal Law, Criminology, and Police Sci. 46: 658-672.

JULIEN, R. (1975) A Primer of Drug Action. San Francisco: Freeman.

KITTRIE, N. (1971) The Right To Be Different. Baltimore: Johns Hopkins Press.

KLEIN, M., K. TEILMANN, J. STYLES, S. LINCOLN, and LABIN-ROSENS-WEIG (1976) "The explosion of police diversion programs," in M. Klein (ed.) The Juvenile Justice System. Beverly Hills, CA: Sage.

KLIR, G. (1972) Trends in General Systems Theory. New York: John Wiley.

KUHN, A. (1975) Unified Social Science. Homewood, IL: Dorsey.

LEWIS, D. and D. BALLA (1976) Delinquency and Psychopathology. New York: Grune & Stratton.

LOEHLIN, J., G. LINDZEY, and J. SPUHLER (1975) Race Differences in Intelligence. San Francisco: Freeman.

MASER, J. and M. SELIGMAN (1977) Psychopathology: Experimental Models. San Francisco: Freeman.

MEDNICK, S. and K. O. CHRISTIANSEN (1977) Biosocial Bases of Criminal Behavior. New York: Gardner.

MICHAEL, J. and M. J. ADLER (1933) Crime, Law and Social Structure. New York: Harcourt, Brace.

MUELLER, G.O.W. (1969) Crime, Law and the Scholars. Seattle: Univ. of Washington Press.

NETTLER, G. (1978) Explaining Crime. New York: McGraw-Hill.

NEWMAN, G. (1978) The Punishment Response. Philadelphia: Lippincott.

OLIVERIO, A. (1977) Genetics, Environment, and Intelligence. New York: Elsevier.

PACKER, H. L. (1968) The Limits of the Criminal Sanction. Stanford, CA: Stanford Univ. Press.

PRIBRAM, K. and M. GILL (1976) Freud's Project Re-Assessed. New York: Basic Books.

RADZINOWICZ, L. (1977) The Growth of Crime. New York: Basic Books.

ROSENTHAL, D. and S. KETY (1968) Transmission of Schizophrenia. New York: Pergamon.

ROTHMAN, D. J. (1971) The Discovery of the Asylum. Boston: Little, Brown.

SARRI, R. and R. VINTER (1976) "Justice for whom?" in M. Klein (ed.) The Juvenile Justice System. Beverly Hills, CA: Sage.

SCOTT, J. F. (1971) Internalization of Norms. Englewood Cliffs, NJ: Prentice-Hall.

SERRILL, M. (1976a) "Critics of corrections speak out." Corrections Magazine 2 (March): 3-8.

—— (1976b) "LEAA: a question of impact." Corrections Magazine 2 (June): 6-12.

STINE, G. (1977) Biosocial Genetics. New York: Macmillan.

U.N. General Assembly (1977) "Crime prevention and control." A/32/199 (September 22): 1-37.

VAN PRAAG, H. M. and J. BRUINVELS (1977) Neurotransmission and Disturbed Behavior. Utrecht: Bohn, Scheltema, & Holkema.

WHITE, S. and S. KRISLOV (1977) Understanding Crime. Washington,DC: National Academy of Sciences.

WILLIAMS, R. (1967) You Are Extraordinary. New York: Random House.

——— and D. KALITA (1977) A Physician Handbook on Orthomolecular Medicine. New York: Pergamon.

WOOTTON, B. (1959) Social Science and Social Policy. New York: Macmillan.

4

CRIMINOLOGICAL THEORY, SOCIAL SCIENCE, AND THE REPRESSION OF CRIME

DONALD R. CRESSEY
University of California, Santa Barbara

the American Society of Criminology presented the Edwin H. Sutherland Award to me on November 4, 1967. I seized the occasion to make two predictions about the future of criminology. The first came out as follows:

> Criminological theorists and administrators of criminal justice alike are beginning to recognize that the process of designating a person as a delinquent or a criminal includes the process of negotiation. I expect that, for this reason, the principal focus of criminological concern during the next decade will be on a phenomenon best characterized by a phrase which, at first glance, appears to contain a contradiction of terms—"negotiated justice." Interdisciplinary study of this phenomenon, perhaps called by a different name, is likely to give criminology an integrated character it has never before experienced [Cressey, 1968: 5-6].

In 1967, of course, no one knew that the Law Enforcement Assistance Administration was going to throw billions into a war on crime or that the so-called "research arm" of LEAA, the National Institute of Law Enforcement and Administration of Justice, was going to be more interested in financing studies of what to do about "the crime problem" than in financing studies about why there is a "crime problem" to worry about. For that matter, there was nothing to suggest that a few scattered college courses in "police science" would blossom into hundreds of programs in "law enforcement" or, in full flower, into university departments and schools granting undergraduate and graduate degrees in "criminal justice science," "criminal justice administration," and "criminology." It is somewhat surprising to find, therefore, that I went on to make another prediction:

> As both lawyers and social scientists become increasingly concerned with negotiated justice as a "problem," a melding of legal knowledge and social science knowledge will occur. Consistently, we should expect the teaching of courses on delinquency and crime, and on the procedures invented for coping with these phenomena, to shift out of departments of sociology and into law schools or into specialized interdisciplinary schools or curricula. . . . This revived interest in the criminal law and its administration will significantly change the content of what has been regarded as "criminology" in the United States [Cressey, 1968: 13-14].

The first prediction was dead wrong. There has been concern for "negotiated justice," but it has hardly become "the principal focus of criminological concern." Instead, the main concern seems to have become that of devising ways to *minimize* negotiations, to do studies and write essays showing that too many criminals are escaping the punitive net which legislators have set for them. For example, a decade ago it seemed that the trend was toward studies of the kind done by four of my recent Ph.D. students—studies suggesting that legislators and executives can never specify in criminal laws and administrative rules just what it is that they want punished, making it necessary for criminal justice workers to negotiate about what the law "really" means (Sanders, 1977; Daudistel, 1976; Williams, 1977; Driscoll, 1977). What has appeared, however, is a plethora of studies and essays purporting to show that if statutes are given a literal reading, thereby minimizing discretionary decision-making, punishments will increase and crime rates will go down. Many of these "rule of law" studies were recently discussed by Platt and Takagi (1977), so it is not necessary to review them here.

The second prediction was much better, on its face. Criminology courses have shifted out of departments of sociology. Professors of law are teaching courses on the criminal law in action, and it is even rumored that some of the new undergraduate departments are offering courses with titles such as "Handcuffs 1A" and "The Miranda Mumble." Clearly, the content of criminology has changed. Nevertheless, the 1967 prediction was not accurate. For example, it mentions a "melding" of legal knowledge and social science knowledge. The expectation was that, among other things, psychological and sociological principles of human learning would increasingly be used in an attempt to understand the behavior of legislators, police officers, judges, and other criminal justice personnel, as well as the behavior of criminals themselves. The "melding" prediction also was based on an expectation that sociological knowledge about the behavior of organizations and institutions—ranging from small bureaucracies to broad political and economic systems—would increasingly be used in systematic efforts to understand the behavior of criminal justice organizations and legal institutions. Neither of these expectations has been fulfilled.

Rather than a *blending* of social science knowledge and legal knowledge, there seems to have been a *smothering* of social science knowledge as criminology has expanded. An exception is econometrics and other statistical methods which seem peculiarly suited to showing that crime rates will decrease if repressive defense measures and repressive tactics of terror are increased. The diminishing influence of social science is anomalous, for theoretical ideas about human learning and social organization, often emanating from the ivory tower, were at the base of many significant criminal justice innovations in the last century, including the juvenile court, the probation system, the parole system, changes in the insanity defense, and changes in the conditions of imprisonment. Scientific curiosity and its offspring, scientific theory, have also been important foundation stones of more recent criminal justice programs. Among them are decriminalizing drunkenness and marijuana use (Schur and Bedau, 1974), enlarging the economic opportunities of youth (Cloward and Ohlin, 1960), diversion of delinquents (Lemert, 1971), and developing a sense of community in urban districts (Rosett and Cressey, 1976).

As we shall see, the smothering of sociological criminology has been part of a predicted change in "the content of what has beed regarded as 'criminology' in the United States." Put succinctly, however, the 1967 prediction did not foresee that criminology would become more and more concerned with increasing the efficiency of the punitive legal apparatus and less and less concerned with trying to discover the processes generating the criminals to be punished and the laws and personnel doing the punishing.

There is an appalling lack of consensus among criminologists regarding even such fundamental problems as definition of subject matter. No academic discipline has a monopoly on criminology. Its nebulous character makes it "interdisciplinary," but this character also opens it up to all comers, including policy technicians, police officers, prison wardens, and other practitioners, some of whom become working university criminologists only after they retire. A nuclear physicist doing scientific work in a laboratory in any nation of the world could quite easily (barring political considerations) transfer the work to a laboratory in another nation, quickly melding it with research being done in the new laboratory. This is not true of contemporary criminologists. Even within the United States, the research being conducted in one center or institute may be completely unrelated to the research being conducted in another, principally because there are wide variations in definitions of the subject matter, in conceptions of criminology's objectives, and—especially—in theory about why people and organizations behave the way they do. These variations, in turn, are related to the fact that persons can become criminologists, or even "criminal justice scientists," simply by declaring that their work is somehow related to crime.

Until the recent expansion, it was proper to say, as Sutherland (1934: 3) said years ago, that criminologists try to develop valid propositions about the processes of making laws, breaking laws, and reaction to the breaking of laws, and about the interrelations among these processes. This emphasis excluded practitioners and other crime fighters. The ideal criminology was an ivory tower, science-oriented, research enterprise rather than a crime fighting coalition. Criminological researchers did not seek propositions for the immediate purpose of "doing something" about crime. They worked in pursuit of truth, not in the pursuit of criminals or, for that matter, in political pursuit of class bias or racial and ethnic bigotry among legislators and criminal justice personnel.

It seems almost obvious that anyone concerned with developing a body of knowledge about the processes of making laws, breaking laws, and reacting to the breaking of laws must be a social scientist. This because criminological ideas must be borrowed from established academic disciplines—especially anthropology, history, psychology, and sociology. If this borrowing does not occur, any "innovative" generalizations are likely to be either crackpot notions about what demons are doing these days or mere recitations of punitive political philosophies espoused in some bygone age. Until about a decade ago, most criminologists—at least most of the good ones—engaged in such borrowing. They were social scientists first and criminologists second. They studied criminological data for the same reason that other social scientists studied data pertaining to child rearing, social stratification, industrial organization, middle class neuroses, and so on—to make a contribution to social science. Malinowski, Freud, Durkheim, Marx, and Weber were all "criminologists" of this kind. But today only a handful of all the persons calling themselves criminologists use social science knowledge to make sense of why legislators, criminals, criminal justice personnel, and legal institutions behave as they behave.

Until recently, also, criminologists repeatedly and systematically asked what causes conduct, whether it be the conduct of legislators who make criminal laws, criminals who break them, or criminal justice personnel who react to breaking of laws. This concern was, and is, related to the objective of developing valid generalizations. A principle of cause and effect is essential to any generalization about why criminal laws are passed. For example, it was a conception of causation that enabled Hall (1935) to make one of the first good studies in the sociology of criminal law, noting that certain changes in economic, political, and social conditions resulted in (that is to say, caused) changes in the law of larceny. Similarly, a principle of cause and effect is essential to any generalization about why laws are broken. For example, it was a conception of causation that enabled Sutherland (1939) to say that criminal behavior results from an excess of associations with criminal behavior patterns, and which enabled Sellin (1938) to say that, historically speaking, high crime rates followed the development of societies characterized by normative conflict. And, finally, a conception of causation is essential to any generalization about why laws are administered in the ways they are administered. For example, it was a conception of causation which made it possible for Aubert (1952) to explain why some laws are not enforced, and, more generally, for Rusche (1933) to explain why punishment of criminals fluctuates.

But contemporary criminology seems to be abandoning cause and effect principles along with the attempt to improve criminological generalizations. In the last decade, a larger and larger proportion of all criminologists, including some sociologists (Matza, 1969; Box, 1971; Tornüdd, 1971; Taylor, Walton, and Young, 1973), seem to have become indifferent or even antagonistic to explanations based on the idea of natural causation. Put in terms used earlier, criminologists seem to be drifting away from making causal sense of criminological data and toward a direct concern for "doing something" about crime. As Wheeler (1976: 525) has pointed out, even sociologists are studying criminal law administration rather than crime and criminals:

Over the past quarter of a century, the concepts we have used to comprehend crime and criminality, and the research we have conducted, have changed. These changes have had two crucial consequences. First, they have led us to focus on those agents and agencies that deal with offenders: the police, the courts, and other way-stations in our system of social control. In the course of this shift, we have been led away from our original point of inquiry, namely, crime, the criminal, and criminality. The result is that we now know far more about those persons whose jobs depend on the existence and importance of crime, than we do about the offenders.

Clearly, criminology has come out of the ivory tower and moved into the policy-making arena. The typical modern criminologist is a technical assistant to politicians bent on repressing crime, rather than a scientist seeking valid propositions stated in a causal framework. If cause—and with it the search for generalizations—goes out the window, criminology will become even more of a hodgepodge than it is now.[1] In the long run, the nation will be worse off as a result. This because, as Platt and Takagi have noted (1977), a decline of interest in the causes of crime leads to penal policy which eliminates sociological considerations from penal procedure, a characteristic of fascist states, not democracies.

Scientists concerned with problems of causation have made important contributions to policy. Indeed, an ancient and honorable scientific principle is that "control" is achieved by first gaining an understanding of the sources (cause) of a phenomenon and then using that knowledge in an attempt to modify the cause. Government policy regarding the control of malaria did not become effective until scientists understood malaria. And those who came to understand malaria were dependent on earlier nineteenth-century scientists who developed the "germ theory" of disease, a set of propositions about the cause of all illness. We are still very far from an understanding which would make it possible to control crime and the criminal justice processes in this scientific sense. As pointed out elsewhere, we have not yet developed an accepted general theory which is comparable to the "germ theory" of disease in scope, let alone derivative theories about the specific conditions causing specific kinds of behavior:

> Although a general theory of criminal behavior and crime, such as the theory of differential association and differential social organization, organizes criminological knowledge and is therefore helpful in making sense of the gross facts about crime, it also is desirable to break crime into more homogeneous units and to develop explanations of these units. In this respect, explaining crime is like explaining disease—development of the germ theory of disease radically altered the approach to illness by making sense of sicknesses which were regarded as the outcome of mere happenstance, or of a wide variety of "factors," including evil spirits. But once germ theory was developed, progress was made, and is being made, by studying specific diseases and specific germs, not by continuing to study the relationship between diseases and germs in general. . . . In criminology, similarly, it seems desirable to continue the development of general theory comparable in scope to germ theory, but it also seems desirable to concentrate research work on specific crimes [such as] burglary, robbery, kidnapping, and rape [Sutherland and Cressey, 1978: 275].

Given the present state of behavioral and social science, and given the present state of politics, there seems to be no current alternative to hit-or-miss attempts at repressive and bureaucratic control of criminals, crime, and criminal justice personnel by legislators. Wilson (1975) has documented this point quite nicely. By analogy, politicians cannot wait for the results of the search for the cause of malaria. They must try to control malaria by condemning night air and by developing a tight bureaucracy that would efficiently keep people indoors at night. They do not know what else to do.

What is disturbing is not the observation that politicians must act without waiting for scientific knowledge to appear, or without waiting for such knowledge to be transformed into action frameworks that policy makers can use (Sutherland and Cressey, 1978: 675-676). The tragedy is in the tendency of modern criminologists to drop the search for causes and to join the politicans. Rather than trying to develop better ideas about why crimes flourish, for example, these criminologists— including Wilson (1975), van den Haag (1975), Ehrlich (1973), Fogel (1975), Morris and Hawkins (1977), and hundreds of others—seem satisfied with a technological criminology whose main concern is for showing policy makers how to repress criminals and criminal justice workers more efficiently. This trend is not without its causes.[2]

First, there is a growing awareness that the variables in some seemingly sound criminological principles, such as differential association and differential social organization, are not readily manipulable and hence are not readily adaptable to interventionist control. Politicians cannot spend money on improved child-rearing practices, as the differential association principle implies they should do. It is in no way possible that the LEAA would fund a demonstration project designed to increase the amount of love in Chicago as a means of reducing the murder rate, also an implication of differential association theory. Similarly, the notion that behavior is learned in a Skinnerian way seems sound enough, but the variables in this principle are not easily manipulable, meaning that policy makers cannot readily use the principle as a foundation for widespread interventionist programs (Wheeler, 1973). Further, more general criminological theories, such as the idea that the capitalistic economy causes misery and misery causes crime (Quinney, 1977), do not contain many variables on which politicians are ready and willing to put our money. It has been easy to conclude, then, that criminologists should revert to the study of how to implement an outdated theory whose variables *are* readily manipulable—the theory that crime is caused by weak repressive measures.

Second, everyone now seems to be observing that certain interventionist policies which were haphazardly based on social science theory did not dramatically reduce criminality and crime, even though much money was spent on them. For instance, Freudian theory invaded correctional agencies years ago, despite protests that, so far as criminality is concerned, the theory is fruitless. Similarly, opportunity (status frustration) theory, with its implication that crime is caused by poverty, made its mark with the Kennedys and other policy makers of the early 1960s. Perhaps these theories became popular in the effort to control crime because their variables are manipulable, not because the theories themselves were considered sound. But, whatever the reason for using them, the recidivism rate and the crime rate continued upward despite these efforts to base crime control policy on social science knowledge. It has therefore been easy for criminologists to conclude that they must study or advocate something more "practical" than social science, namely repression.

Disillusionment with social science, then, seems to be a current criminological fad, and this cynicism seems to have had punitive consequences. Criminologists, like politicians, are saying that our efforts to change criminals and the society that produces them have been ineffective and that we must therefore retain punishment and abandon the effort to understand criminals and society and then do something about changing them. For example, it even has become fashionable for liberal organizations, such as the American Friends Service Committee (1971) and the Twentieth Century Fund (1976), to announce that the rehabilitative ideal—as it pertains to *criminals*—has failed, that criminals suffer under it, and that politicians therefore should return to the policies of the classical school of criminology. Similarly, it has become fashionable to announce that the rehabilitative ideal—as it pertains to *society*—has failed, and that powerful persons should therefore routinely continue to punish blacks, poor people, and a few others, rather than trying to seek out and modify the social systems generating high crime rates (Wilson, 1974; van den Haag, 1975; Morris and Hawkins, 1977).

Until about a decade ago, of course, most criminologists were arguing that repression is neither scientifically nor democratically sound and that therefore the effort to understand the conditions spawning crime and criminals should be enlarged. David Bazelon, Chief Judge of the U.S. Court of Appeals for the District of Columbia, recently joined these science-oriented criminologists. He warned that when the study of crime causation is ignored, repressive measures flourish:

> Today street crime has replaced anarchism and communism as our cause for alarm. . . . And in the legislatures there is a rush to adopt tougher sentencing provisions. The spirit of our response to previous demons can be discerned in our reaction to the crime threat.
>
> Our libertarian tradition would tell us to get tough with the "deprivations that caused the disease" rather than with those who manifest the symptoms.
>
> Mandatory incarceration, determinate sentencing, and the like are the first steps in a thousand-mile journey, but in precisely the wrong direction: towards repression. Mandatory incarceration means nothing more than locking up those manifesting symptoms of the underlying ill. If it reduces crime, and it probably can, it will only be because repression and fear can be effective [quoted by Bennet, 1976; see also Bazelon, 1977].

Modern criminology would benefit if contemporary criminologists put Judge Bazelon's plea for policy based on knowledge of "the underlying ill" into historical perspective. Until about a century ago, there were few alternatives to the punitive reaction to crime. The politicians and philosophers of criminology's classical school routinely assumed that criminals simply choose to be bad and will choose to change their ways if they are punished severely enough. Consistently, leaders of this classical school routinely assumed that severe punishment of criminals will deter potential criminals, thus keeping the crime rate low. Nothing approaching a psychology of criminals or a sociology of crime was imaginable because the notion of natural causation had not yet been applied to human conduct. The classical theorists believed in "free will" and therefore could be concerned only with helping policy makers be more efficient—that is, more repressive. Because there was no psychology of criminals or sociology of law, crime, or administration, state officials had the apparent choice of trying to terrorize the citizenry into conformity or doing nothing about the "crime problem." An empty headed, know-nothing criminology which makes no long-run effort to change these alternatives, and toward which contemporary criminologists seem to be plunging, is what Judge Bazelon is implicitly attacking.

To elaborate a bit, it seems clear that, in the last hundred years, criminologists and others first invented and then developed an alternative to punitive policies. They broke away from a criminology which assumed that it had the God-given truth. They helped develop the notion of natural causation in human events, and in doing so they made it possible to try to control criminality and crime by cutting off their roots. Some of the theories on which interventionist policies were based turned out to be silly, just as other scientific ideas turned out to be silly as new discoveries were made. For example, the biological determinism theory of criminal conduct went down the tube long ago, though there are periodic attempts to revive it. More recently, the popular "emotional disturbances" theory also started sliding down the tube, and with it the medical model for "treating" criminals. Decades ago, research by sociological criminologists concluded that this theory about the causation of criminal behavior is based on a misconception of the nature of "personality." Sutherland's research on white-collar crime (1949) seemed to clinch this point. Nevertheless, government officials modified punitive policy to fit "emotional disturbances" theory, probably because the theory found something wrong with criminals and nothing wrong with the social order. Criminal justice personnel started using an approach called "treatment," even when the help given offenders consisted merely of finding them jobs, teaching them arithmetic, or relaxing prison discipline. Now, most criminologists agree that this alternative to punitive policy was based on poor science, comparable to the poor science that discovered night air to be the cause of malaria. But only a few of these criminologists are trying to develop alternative causal theory. They are not even arguing for retention of the humane handling of criminals which was justified on the ground that humanitarianism is "treatment" (Cressey, 1960).

But the failure of "emotional disturbances" theory should not be taken as evidence that scientific criminology should be abandoned or even smothered. For almost half a century this theory and the medical model based on it distracted from an alternative scientific generalization mentioned earlier, namely the principle that criminality and crime are caused by the kind of social organization characterizing modern industrialized nations (Sutherland, 1939; Sutherland and Cressey, 1978). One alternative for contemporary criminologists is that of turning to this sociological model, making its variables manipulable, and developing it into a stronger foundation for the kind of interventionist policy Judge Bazelon admires. A second alternative is to develop different scientific principles, to find new explanations of criminality and crime by studying the conditions under which persons become criminals and the conditions under which crime rates rise. But most criminologists seem indifferent to both alternatives. They are giving their research and scholarly attention to improving the efficiency of repressive efforts, apparently assuming (correctly) that if the state is repressive enough, most people will stop doing what lawmakers do not want them to do, and apparently assuming (incorrectly) that intervention policy based on science is impossible.

An appreciation of the important implications of these two assumptions, and of what seems to be happening in criminology, may be had by looking briefly at the differences between three distinct "new criminologies," one of them a half-century old, the others quite recent. They represent alternative pathways for contemporary criminology.

In the 1920s, biologists were excited about the possible effects of the endocrine or ductless glands on personality and personal conduct. Inevitably, the idea that people's destinies are determined by their juices was transformed into a criminological theory. One book claimed that its glandular theory of crime would account for all of the discrepancies, errors, oversights, and inadequacies of other theories (Schlapp and Smith, 1928: 72). Significantly, the book was called *The New Criminology*. Endocrinologists laughed at it. So did most of the few criminologists who were around at the time. Apparently no crime control policy was based on this scientific idea about why people behave the way they behave.

More recently, three young English gentlemen gave us *The New Criminology: For a Social Theory of Deviance* (Taylor, Walton, and Young, 1973). They, like Schlapp and Smith, asked analysts of criminal law, crime, criminals, and criminal justice programs to ignore most of what had gone on before. Despite the title of the book, the request is for an abolition of criminology. Sociologists are to drop *sociological* theory and concentrate on *social* theory, thus addressing themselves to "the wider origins of the deviant act," to dealing with "the society as a totality," and to concerning themselves with the question of "man's relationship to structures of power, domination and authority—and the ability of men to confront these structures in acts of crime, deviance, and dissent" (Taylor, Walton, and Young, 1973: 268-278). The authors advocate, in other words, that intellectuals do more of what the authors do in their book, which they review in one long sentence:

> With Marx, we have been concerned with the social arrangements that have obstructed, and the social contradictions that enhance, man's chances of achieving full sociality—a state of freedom from material necessity, and (therefore) of material incentive, a release from the constraints of forced production, an abolition of the forced division of labor, and a set of social arrangements, therefore, in which there would be no politically, economically, and socially-induced need to criminalize deviance [Taylor, Walton, and Young, 1973: 270].

The third, and most recent, "new criminology" stresses repression in the form of defense and deterrence. It was given its name by James Q. Wilson, the political scientist who almost single-handedly made research on police a respectable social science enterprise (Wilson, 1968). But in recent years Wilson has seemed more interested in making police officers efficient than understanding their behavior. In an introduction to a book written by a retired policeman, Wilson (1974: xv) describes a "new criminology" as follows:

> There is slowly arising a "new criminology" to supplement traditional criminology. To a large extent, crime has traditionally been studied from the point of view of the criminal (trying to discover what "causes" him or her to commit illegal acts), in ways that treat crime as a general and undifferentiated phenomenon (for example, any kind of "juvenile delinquency," or all the components of the FBI Crime Index), and only with limited concern for specific policies that might be effective in reducing crime. There are of course conspicuous exceptions—one thinks of Marvin Wolfgang's study of murder—but the prevailing pattern has been based on an intellectual orientation toward describing the incidence or explaining the causes of generalized forms of social deviance. The new criminology—not literally new, of course, for there has always been some work in this vein—considers crime from the point of view of the victim, treats particular kinds of offenses (e.g.,

residential burglaries, stranger-to-stranger assaults), and considers explicitly the effectiveness of alternative prevention strategies.

Of the three "new criminologies," the third seems to best signal the direction in which criminology is turning. It makes "prevention strategies" into that which local chiefs of police must have in mind when they, during Crime Prevention Week, tell the members of the Kiwanis Club to lock their cars and to stop newspaper deliveries when on vacation. These officers are defenders. It is not part of their job to study the underlying processes by which the community is generating criminals to be defended against, what Judge Bazelon calls "the underlying ill." Wilson notes that all criminologists have not become as empty headed as police chiefs. His "new criminology" merely *supplements* "traditional criminology," the kind which tries, among other things, to understand crime and then to base policy on this understanding, thus making defense (and control by terror) unnecessary in the long run. But he also makes that which is being supplemented, the long-range scientific approach to crime control, look as though it were just a useless and misguided "intellectual orientation toward describing the incidence or explaining the causes of generalized forms of social deviance." By analogy, he would not have wanted nineteenth-century biologists to pay so much attention to germs. A "new biology" comparable to his "new criminology" would have asked biologists to develop more efficient techniques for blood letting, the known "cure" for all diseases. What Wilson does not seem to appreciate is the fact that his "supplement" is not an atheoretical concern for "the effectiveness of alternative prevention strategies." It is a theoretical position, one calling for policy based on the eighteenth-century hedonistic psychology of Jeremy Bentham and his contemporaries. By using the term "new criminology" to describe an ancient and outmoded approach, Wilson is asking criminologists to stay out of ivory towers and to join him and other "new realists" (Platt and Takagi, 1977) in repressive battles against residential burglary, assaults, and so on. If more and more criminologists respond—and they seem to be doing so—criminology will eventually have only a "Handcuffs 1A" orientation.

The "new criminology" of the young English gentlemen goes to the opposite extreme. Its originators ask neither for studies which would improve defensive repression or studies which would improve stratagems of terror (general deterrence and specific deterrence). The have an interventionist orientation, but nevertheless tell social scientists to drop the idea of natural causation. Their aim is to replace traditional criminology, not to supplement it. Taylor, Walton, and Young (1973: 31-66, 128) assert that past biological, psychological, and sociological work on the processes of making laws, breaking laws, and reacting to breaking laws is irrelevant because it sought natural causes. Their approach is antiscientific. It insists, with Jeremy Bentham and with James Q. Wilson and other "new realists," that individuals are self-determining, that they have a "free will." Scientific generalizations about human behavior—as well as about the specific behaviors of legislators, criminals, and criminal justice personnel—are impossible if one does not make the observation that humans start out as empty vessels who are programmed (caused) to behave by their milieux, like all other animals. But Taylor, Walton, and Young seem to have an aversion to this scientific conception. Their "new criminology" consistently asks sociologists and psychologists to forget about science (positivism), to worry about how and why capitalism arose, and to help raise the consciousness levels of people beneath them in class status. This admirable call for intellectualism inadvertently leaves criminology, as such, to those who, in the words of Platt and Takagi (1977: 12), have "a grim determination to hold the line and add new fortifications to the garrison state."

The first "new criminology," which saw our destiny in glands, was both arrogant and erroneous. Nevertheless, it was based on the scientific principle that crime control should depend on knowledge rather than on defense and terror. By implication, it ásserted that criminologists should shake the shackles of the classical school and keep trying to locate the conditions which cause persons to behave criminally, thus providing a basis for policies which would try to modify these conditions. An innovative, reckless, and even wasteful "new criminology" also is implied, in contrast with Wilson's safe, conservative, technological, bureaucratic "new criminology." Further, an empirical criminology is implied, in contrast with the speculative or philosophical enterprise advocated by Taylor, Walton, and Young. So far as control is concerned, positive, constructive, programs are called for, in contrast to the negative but nevertheless popular programs of defense and deterrence which flow from the free will assumption.

Schlapp and Smith's "new criminology" was done in by other science-oriented "new criminologies." "Emotional disturbances" theory was a "new criminology" of this kind, although no one gave it that name.[3] As suggested earlier, this kind of theory will soon be as outdated as "ductless gland" theory. There is a great need for new generalizations which will make sense of criminological data. Someone must develop them. It is 1978, and the criminal law theory of the twentieth century has not yet been written. Our criminal law is based on eighteenth-century psychological theory. Our political leaders seem bent on applying this eighteenth-century stuff—which was introduced into criminal law as a means of *reducing* punishments—with a vengeance.

Criminologists should not abandon science to become policy advisors in this repressive war on crime. Neither should they retreat into broad intellectualizing, accompanied by political proselytizing. They might well be advised to take up low paying posts in ivory towers, monasteries, and similar think-tanks. There, they should sharpen their scientific research tools and put them to work on studies designed to secure comprehension of the conditions under which criminal laws are enacted, enforced, and broken. If they do so, and come up with some reasonable generalizations, politicians might listen to them, just as politicians listened to Bentham, Beccaria, Voltaire, and even Freud.

NOTES

1. None of this is meant to imply that criminologists who produce statistical correlations are not good criminologists. I have no quarrel with scientists who correlate repressive legislation, or crime rates, or imprisonment rates, on the one hand, and social conditions such as unemployment on the other. Indeed, I have just supervised an excellent study along these lines (Jankovic, 1977a, 1977b). I have no quarrel, either, with criminologists (there seem to be hundreds of them) who do multivariate analyses of sentencing practices. I merely note that such correlations and statistical analyses do not by themselves lead to generalizations about the processes of making laws, breaking laws, and reacting to law breaking.

2. Platt and Takagi (1977: 13) attribute the rise of "intellectuals for law and order" to the changing form of class relations and the "class struggle" in the United States. While there is merit in such causal analysis, I shall here restrict myself to discussion of causes *within* criminology.

3. The term "new penology" rather than "new criminology" apparently was extensively used in the 1930s to describe this theory. A textbook discussed "the new penology" at some length, describing it as a system in which prisoners are diagnosed and treated rather than punished (Barnes and Teeters, 1945: 646).

REFERENCES

American Friends Service Committee (1971) Struggle for Justice. New York: Hill & Wang.

AUBERT, V. (1952) "White-collar crime and social structure." Amer. J. of Sociology 58: 263-271.

BARNES, H. E. and N. K. TEETERS (1945) New Horizons in Criminology. New York: Prentice-Hall.

BAZELON, D. L. (1977) "Street crime and correctional potholes." Federal Probation 41: 1-9.

BENNET, S. A. (1976) "A bicentennial inquiry into American law." Trial 12: 16-33.

BOX, S. (1971) Deviance, Reality, and Society. London: Holt, Rinehart & Winston.

CLOWARD, R. A. and L. E. OHLIN (1960) Delinquency and Opportunity: A Theory of Delinquent Gangs. Glencoe, IL: Free Press.

CRESSEY, D. R. (1968) "Negotiated justice." Criminologica 5: 5-16.

——— (1960) "Limitation on organization of treatment in the modern prison," in R. A. Cloward et al., Theoretical Studies in Social Organization of the Prison. New York: Social Science Research Council.

DAUDISTEL, H. E. (1976) "Deciding what the law means: an examination of police-prosecutor discretion." Unpublished Ph.D. dissertation, University of California, Santa Barbara.

DRISCOLL, J. P. (1977) "No one to count cadence: the police officer as law maker." Unpublished Ph.D. dissertation, University of California, Santa Barbara.

EHRLICH, I. (1973) "Participation in illegitimate activities: a theoretical and empirical investigation." J. of Pol. Economy 81: 521-565.

FOGEL, D. (1975) We Are the Living Proof: The Justice Model for Corrections. Cincinnati: W. H. Anderson.

HALL, J. (1935) Theft, Law and Society. Boston: Little, Brown.

JANKOVIC, I. (1977a) "Punishment and the post-industrial society: a study of unemployment, crime and imprisonment in the United States." Unpublished Ph.D. dissertation, University of California, Santa Barbara.

——— (1977b) "Labor market and imprisonment." Crime and Social Justice 8: 17-31.

LEMERT, E. M. (1971) Instead of Court: Diversion in Juvenile Justice. Washington, DC: Government Printing Office.

MATZA, D. (1969) Becoming Deviant. Englewood Cliffs, NJ: Prentice-Hall.

MORRIS, N. and G. HAWKINS (1977) Letter to the President on Crime Control. Chicago: Univ. of Chicago Press.

PLATT, T. and P. TAKAGI (1977) "Intellectuals for law and order: a critique of the new 'realists'." Crime and Social Justice 8: 1-16.

QUINNEY, R. (1977) Class, State and Crime: On the Theory and Practice of Criminal Justice. New York: David McKay.

ROSETT, A. I. and D. R. CRESSEY (1976) Justice By Consent: Plea Bargains in the American Courthouse. Philadelphia: Lippincott.

RUSCHE, G. (1933) "Arbeitsmarkt und Strafvollung." Zeitschrift für Sozialforschung 2: 63-78.

SANDERS, W. B. (1977) Detective Work: A Study of Criminal Investigations. New York: Free Press.

SCHLAPP, M. G. and E. H. SMITH (1928) The New Criminology. New York: Boni.

SCHUR, E. M. and H. A. BEDAU (1974) Victimless Crimes: Two Sides of a Controversy. Englewood Cliffs, NJ: Prentice-Hall.

SELLIN, T. (1938) Culture Conflict and Crime. New York: Social Science Research Council.

SUTHERLAND, E. H. (1949) White Collar Crime. New York: Dryden.

——— (1939) Principles of Criminology. (Third edition.) Philadelphia: Lippincott.

——— (1934) Principles of Criminology. (Second edition.) Philadelphia: Lippincott.

——— and D. R. CRESSEY (1978) Criminology. (Tenth edition.) Philadelphia: Lippincott.

TAYLOR, I., P. WALTON, and J. YOUNG (1973) The New Criminology: For a Social Theory of Deviance. London: Routledge & Kegan Paul.

TORNUDD, P. (1971) "The futility of searching for causes of crime." Scandinavian Studies in Criminology 3: 23-33.

Twentieth Century Fund Task Force on Criminal Sentencing (1976) Fair and Certain
    Punishment. New York: McGraw-Hill.
VAN DEN HAAG, E. (1975) Punishing Criminals: Concerning a Very Old and
    Painful Question. New York: Basic Books.
WHEELER, H. [ed.] (1973) Beyond the Punitive Society. San Francisco: W. H.
    Freeman.
WHEELER, S. (1976) "Trends and problems in the sociological study of crime."
    Social Problems 23: 525-534.
WILLIAMS, M. L. (1977) "Playing it by ear: the functions of typified knowledge
    in police patrol." Unpublished Ph.D. dissertation, University of California,
    Santa Barbara.
WILSON, J. Q. (1975) Thinking About Crime. New York: Basic Books.
———(1974) "Foreword," to T. A. Reppetto, Residential Crime. Cambridge, MA:
    Ballinger.
———(1968) Varieties of Police Behavior: The Management of Law and Order in
    Eight Communities. Cambridge, MA: Harvard Univ. Press.

5

CHANGE AND STABILITY IN
CRIMINAL JUSTICE

MARVIN E. WOLFGANG
University of Pennsylvania

We are all deeply concerned with the problems of crime and criminal justice, the layman and the criminologist. We who count ourselves as criminologists are the heirs of the diligent scholarship of giants such as Thorsten Sellin, Edwin Sutherland, Herman Mannheim, Robert Merton, Sir Leon Radzinowicz; and we carry in our own persons the traditions of perspective and philosophy that invoke a special concern with crime and punishment, a concern more focused than that of others not exposed to our training. Our perspectives and our concerns change with experience, learning, training, and with changes in the climate of the country and the world, political and intellectual. As a contemporary witness to those traditions, I have undergone some of the changes that are part of the perspectives I wish to document briefly here.

Overall, one of the major theses of change has been a movement that can be associated with the names of two pioneers in American sociological thought. It is a movement from the approach of William Graham Sumner of description without prescription, to the social philosophy of Lester Ward, from which social policy was derived and promulgated. It is a movement from simply announcing empirically derived scien-

AUTHOR'S NOTE: *An earlier version of this paper was presented as a commencement address at Northeastern University, Boston, June 17, 1978.*

61

tific discovery to that of pronouncing behavioral science conclusions that address political and ethical issues.

Personally, I was brought into some of this change (but not entirely changed) by my position as research director of the National Commission on the Causes and Prevention of Violence, a commission established by President Johnson shortly after the assassination of Senator Robert Kennedy in 1968. The commission was requested by Congress and the President not only to present the best available scientific evidence about conditions of violence but also to recommend broad and specific social changes to reduce it. Moreover, as the Legal Defense Fund of the National Association for the Advancement of Colored People asked me to research the matter of racial discrimination in the sentencing patterns in rape and capital punishment and as I came to testify in federal court on these issues, beginning in 1966, I was forced to make social policy conclusions that used the scientific research evidence. After hours of testimony, my concluding statements invariably became constitutional, ethical, philosophic imperatives that were built upon but transcended scientific, positivistic research; that is, differential sentencing can be translated into racial discrimination, for in statistically significant proportions, more blacks are sentenced to death than whites, even when controlling for 28 significant legal and extralegal variables.

Even with such seemingly basic or pure research that I did with my mentor, Thorsten Sellin, in reaching for a more refined measurement of crime than the FBI crime index and promoting a seriousness score for each kind of crime, I came to the same conclusion that Cesare Beccaria offered in 1764 in his famous essay, *Dei delitti e delle pene (Of Crime and Punishment)*, namely, that the punishment should be proportional, or equal, to the crime. The imperative "should be" did not appear in the 1964 publication, but by 1974 I was willing to use it.

How simple, yet profound, this shift from a medical model that viewed criminals as sick to a justice model that views them as bad. The eighteenth century return of the rational man I have called the neoclassical revival. I accept it and I have advised it before congressional committees and in court testimony.

This change from a passive recipient of data to an active adviser of criminal justice policy has been a dramatic alteration of my personal posture as well as that which criminology in general seems to represent.

The significant change in criminal justice philosophy was, I think, the result of two quite different approaches to the monumental issues of crime and punishment. Both of them began to affect my own perspective many years ago. One was ethical; the other, empirical.

The American Friends Service Committee (1971), a Quaker group, published *Struggle for Justice*, a major document in which the group raised serious issues about the disparity in judicial sentencing, about the inequities of the indeterminate sentence, and many other dissimilarities. Francis Allen, Herbert Packer, Caleb Foote, and others had written and spoken earlier about these same issues of inequity. But *Struggle for Justice* dramatically and clearly laid before us the claims of the rehabilitation model and its ethical deficiencies in a consolidated way that we previously had not experienced. We were told that there were injustices about the approach that put the decision for disposition of criminal offenders on the shoulders of psychologists and psychiatrists who could not adequately discern future dangerousness. We were told that prediction of the future is not an apropriate basis for determining how long an offender should remain in custody. These were ethical issues of equity, and they began to shake many of us out of our mode of thinking about crime and punishment.

Contemporaneous with this ethical arousal was the emergence of empirical evidence that raised serious skepticism about the validity of the treatment, reformation, rehabilitative model.

The American Prison Association first met in Cincinnati in 1870 and pronounced that reformation was the primary purpose of the penal system. This pronouncement was a culmination of earlier Quaker philosophy that built the Eastern State Penitentiary in 1829, of the writings of Isaac Ray and his *Treatise on Medical Jurisprudence* (1838). In the twentieth century, Freud added to this approach and to the apparent tautology that criminals commit crime because they are sick, and criminality is a form of sickness. These propositions helped to initiate criminology into a conviction about the value and virtue of the medical model.

The liturgy, which I espoused in my first teaching of criminology in 1948, was like this: People commit crime because they are emotionally disturbed. Neither legislators who write criminal statutes nor judges who pronounce sentence can know when criminals are reformed and ready to return to society. Therefore, the clinicians of crime—psychiatrists, psychologists, psychiatric social workers—should be given the authority, by the institutional practices of probation, presentence investigation, and parole to determine when the patient-criminal is sufficiently rehabilitated to be released from social control. Thus was born the indefinite and indeterminate sentence: the one-day-to-life and the minimum-maximum models. Thus was born also the coercive, manipulative control and the psychic invasion of prisoners.

But empirical evidence joined the ethical evocations that questioned this philosophy. The more sophisticated the research of evaluation became, the more firm and singular the conclusion that little or none of the rehabilitation programs made much or any difference in the rates of criminal recidivism. In the United States, Sweden, Finland, England, and Norway the conclusions became the same as research accumulated from the late 1960s to the mid-1970s.

There are many ramifications of this criminal justice change in philosophy. They include but are not exhaustive of the following ideas of change.

First, *Treatment to punishment.* The position now taken says that criminals should be punished for what they have done, and in a democracy this means restriction of liberty, reduction of mobility of life space, either in the normal community or in a place called a prison. Neither individual intrapsychic nor group therapy has functioned well to reduce criminality. The purpose of social control of those who harm others is to reconfirm society's moral sentiments against harm by punishment, as Emile Durkheim earlier suggested, which is meant to produce a homeostasis, to equalize the hurt to the offender for the harm he has done to others.

This correspondence between the degree of harm of the crime and the degree of severity of the sanction is now being reemphasized in writings, research, and legislation. We call it the "just deserts" model.

However, I wish to remind you that these ideas reach far back in Western civilization. Hellenic society was not alone in the ancient world in possessing much of this rationale, for the Hammurabic Code in the nineteenth century B.C. and the Mosaic *lex talionis* shared similar notions. Still, Plato (427-347 B.C.) expressed not only the ideal Magnesian society but what Athens probably had. He said in Book 9 of Laws: "But if anyone seems to deserve a greater penalty, let him undergo a long and public imprisonment and be dishonored. . . . No criminal shall go unpunished, not even for a single offense . . . *let the penalty be according to his deserts*" (emphasis added).

Plato would have sounded quite modern if he had testified before the Senate Judiciary Committee in the mid- or later years of the 1970s to discuss S. 1437, the bill to reform the Federal Criminal Code. For Plato had many centuries earlier written in Book 11 of Laws:

> When a man does another any injury by theft or violence, for the greater injury let him pay greater damages to the injured man, and less for the smaller injury; but in all cases, whatever the injury may have been, as much as will compensate the loss.

And besides the compensation of the wrong, let a man pay a
further penalty for the chastisement of his offense: he who has
done the wrong mitigated by the folly of another, through the
lightheartedness of youth or the like, shall pay a lighter
penalty; but he who has injured another through his own folly,
when overcome by pleasure or pain, in cowardly fear, or lust, or
envy, or implacable anger, shall endure a heavier punishment.
. . . The law, like a good archer, should aim at the *right measure
of punishment,* and in all cases at the *deserved punishment*
[emphasis added].

Deterrence was also important to the Hellenic world. The
writers were future oriented both in terms of deterring others
and, as we shall later see, in terms of "purification," as they
called it, or reformation.

Protagoras (481-411 B.C.) said that "he who desires to inflict
rational punishment . . . has regard to the future and is desirous
that the man who is punished, and he who sees him punished
may be deterred from wrong doing again. He punishes for the
sake of prevention, thereby clearly implying that virtue is
capable of being taught" (cited in Kagan, 1965: 145).

Socrates (470-399 B.C.) believed that "the object of all
punishment which is rightly inflicted should be either to
improve and benefit the subject or else to make him an example
to others, who will be deterred by the sight of his sufferings
and reform their own conduct" (cited in Sellin, 1976: 13).

Demosthenes (384?-322 B.C.) told us: "For there are two
objects for which all laws are framed—to deter any man from
doing what is wrong and, by punishing the transgressor,
to make the rest better men" (cited in Kagan, 1965: 141).

Still, the deterrent effect of punishment was questioned even
in Athens. My respected colleague and mentor, Thorsten
Sellin, in *Slavery and the Penal System* (1976), records that
"the Mityleneans had revolted against Athens in 427 B.C. and
Cleon, a leading member of the assembly, had demanded that
a punitive expedition be dispatched with orders to execute all
the rebels as a warning to potential rebels." But, in opposition, Diodotus questioned the deterrent value. He said:

As long as poverty gives men the courage of necessity, or plenty fills them with the ambition which belongs to insolence and pride, and the other conditions of life remain each under the thralldom of some fatal and master passion, so long will the impulse never be wanting to drive men into danger. . . . In fine, it is impossible to prevent . . . human nature doing what it has once set its mind upon, by force of law or by any other deterrent force whatever. We must not, therefore, commit ourselves to a false policy through a belief in the efficiency of the punishment of death, or exclude rebels from the hope of repentance and an early atonement of their errors [cited in Sellin, 1976: 13-14].

Second, *Prediction to retribution.* Predicting crime and delinquency or probation and parole success is a normal pursuit of scientific research. But whether first graders or first offenders will become delinquent or future offenders is no longer a part of criminal justice policy. We should not restrain nor restrict persons on the basis of a prediction of future dangerousness. We restrain and restrict on the basis of past dangerousness, previous violent and harmful behavior. Retribution becomes once more acceptable, not as social revenge but as a matter of social justice.

Third, *Indeterminate to determinate sentences.* The enormous inequities inflicted on offenders by reason of the wide range of judicial discretion previously permitted in the statutes can and should be reduced by providing for presumptive sentencing that establishes clear and firm guidelines for proportional sentencing that makes the punishment fit the crime equally for all persons who commit like crimes.

Fourth, *Coercion to voluntarism.* The right to treatment is joined to the right not to be treated. No longer should therapy, counseling, group treatment, or other programs be required for release from restraint. Treatment programs should be available to all who want them but not because the prison or parole authorities demand them.

Fifth, *Remedies to rights.* Neither the body by corporal punishment nor the mind by drugs or psychic probing should be invaded by coercive therapy. The convicted, and especially the imprisoned, offender needs the protection which civil rights, due process of the Fourteenth Amendment, and avoidance of cruel and unusual punishment of the Eighth Amendment all provide.

Early in the nineteenth century the Philadelphia Quakers, the elite leaders, introduced at the old prison in Cherry Hill what came to be known as the Pennsylvania, or separate, system. In that prison all inmates, all convicts, were kept in solitary confinement from the moment they arrived until the moment they left the institution. With humanitarian intentions to promote self-reformation and to eliminate the effects of social contamination from other convicts, this philosophy and correctional movement were imposed on the criminal justice system and enforced, as Rousseau would force men to be free, on the unfortunates caught in a network of the administration of criminal law.

Charles Dickens (1842) visited the famous Philadelphia prison on his trip to America. At first he was complimentary, but when he put his impressions into writing he was very critical, and his perspective is as current as the critics of today who are opposed to coercive therapy:

> In its intention I am well convinced that it is kind, humane and meant for reformation; but I am persuaded that those who devised the system and those benevolent gentlemen who carry it into execution do not know what it is they are doing. . . . I hold this slow and daily tampering with the mysteries of the brain to be immeasurably worse than any torture of the body; and because its ghastly signs and tokens are not so palpable to the eye and sense of touch as scars upon the flesh, because its wounds are not on the surface, and it extorts few cries that human ears can hear; therefore I denounce it as a secret punishment which slumbering humanity is not roused to stay. [cited in Eriksson, 1976: 70]

There are other issues which I shall not delineate but which have been part of the change in criminology and criminal justice. We now rarely discuss causes but regularly refer to correlates and determinants of crime. Our statistics of probabilities caution us against cause but reinforce John Stuart Mill's terms of association. This behavioral science approach suggests that we react to correlative consequences and seek to alter known effects rather than reach into the enormous chain of variables from proximate to first cause. This is the same kind of change noted in private psychiatric practice: the reduction of psychoanalytic probing of cause to cognitive therapy of current effects.

Moreover, although the social environment remains predominant in all of our investigations about crime and criminality, we are returning to research and theory about biology, physiology, endocrinology, and genetics. There should be no fear that such studies will be dangerous to any ethnic group, for perinatal trauma, protein and other nutritional deficiencies, and postnatal neglect are all elements of environmental control. The relationship between these conditions and crime are now under scrutiny and deserve our research attention.

I have emphasized the changes that have occurred in the philosophy of science and criminal justice, especially during one's years of education in these matters. But I wish also to stress the abiding values which both science and ethics have always maintained.

The first is the scientific method. Karl Pearson, the great statistician who gave us the correlation coefficient, once said that the unity of all science lies not in its matter but in its method, that everything that exists exists in some quantity—heat, light, sound, life, love, justice. No matter what criminal justice philosophy one possesses, it is necessary to measure its consequences by the best available empirical evidence. Truth and reality are our lovely Platonic abstractions; empiricism is our best approximation of them, based on our sensory observations. One must not yield to the rhetoric of fascinating philosophy that has no empirical foundation, but must demand the logic of hypothesis testing and clear definitions of scientific inquiry.

Finally, whatever the position and philosophy of criminal justice, there should always be a concern for the humanity and dignity of the individual. It is true, of course, that some of the worst social inventions were claimed to be concerned with the individual. We must all beware these exhortations. When any social policy claims it is doing something *to* an individual *for* his own good, let us question that policy. Under such circumstances, it is better to be an advocate of the individual, his liberties and rights, than to adopt a broad collective social stance. For the individual—the singular human being—requires protection from the macrosocial forces that surround him. It has been the wisdom of our democracy, especially of the Supreme Court, that has slowly and carefully constructed a Constitution, statutes, case law that protect the individual against false accusations, and, when accused of crime, against the hasty, heavy hand of the behemoth. Consider the magnitude, if not always the majesty, of forces which the state brings to bear upon the offender—the police machinery and organization, prosecutory investigation and discretion, the courts and the penal system. It is not merely the cumulative collection of protective provisions for the accused that the state has created to which I refer. Beneath the institutional safeguards against excessive force and unwarranted intervention there are the attitudes, conduct, modes of interaction of the agents of social control, those who work in what we call our criminal justice system. Functionaries in this system, whatever their role may be, must not lose sight of the rights required and the dignity, not to be denied, of each individual, no matter how heinous the crime nor how much condemned one thinks the criminal should be. In the complexity of our civilization, with alienation and anomie not far from us, with bureaucracies interlocking around us, we are all treacherously close to the edge of our own humanity.

In some occupations, such as nursing, medicine, psychiatry, pediatrics, the clergy, there is meant to be an inherent concern for the individual. But when the clients are not sick, helpless, children, or part of the gospel's flock, when the clients are accused of crime or condemned by society, convicted by our courts, it is especially important that those who work in criminal justice maintain their continued awareness of the individual qua individual rather than viewing those passing through the system as simply segmental pieces of personalities.

The same may be said about the scientific study of criminality. When persons are punched on cards and put on computer tape, we could lose the individual behind the digit. But I have fortunately found that those who work with criminal statistics are as much humanists and as much concerned with the individual as those persons who work in English literature or medieval French.

In either case—in criminology and criminal justice—the individual remains our primary concern. Criminal justice above all is an abiding concern, for us as it was for Socrates and Plato, a concern that will affect and be affected by criminologists throughout our lives.

REFERENCES

American Friends Service Committee (1971) Struggle for Justice. New York: Hill & Wang.

BECCARIA, C. (1764) Dei delitti e delle pene. Many eds. in English.

DICKENS, C. (1842) American Notes for General Circulation. London: Chapman & Hall.

ERIKSSON, T. (1976) The Reformers: An Historical Survey of Pioneer Experiments in the Treatment of Criminals. New York: Elsevier.

KAGAN, D. [ed.] (1965) Sources in Greek Political Thought from Homer to Polybius. New York: Free Press.

PLATO. Laws. Many eds.

PLATO. Gorgias. Many eds.

RAY, I. (1838) A Treatise on the Medical Jurisprudence of Insanity. Boston: Little, Brown; reprinted, 1962, Cambridge: Harvard Univ. Press.

SELLIN, T. (1976) Slavery and the Penal System. New York: Elsevier.

THUCYDIDES (1910 ed.) History of the Peloponnesian War (Richard Crawley, trans.). London: J. M. Dent & Sons.

6

THE LEGALIZATION OF DEVIANCE

JEROME H. SKOLNICK
JOHN DOMBRINK
University of California, Berkeley

mericans wagered more than $17 billion in 1974—on lotteries, horse racing, bingo, legalized numbers, and casino games—in the more than 40 states that permit one form or another of legal gambling (Commission on Gambling, 1976: 77). The liquor industry produced a billion gallons of alcoholic beverages in 1976, on which $5.5 billion in taxes was collected by the government (U.S. Treasury Department, 1978). One third of the adult citizens of the United States were able to light up a joint, fearing, in most cases, the maximum penalty of a $100 citation for that activity (Brownell, 1977). Consenting adults in California were able to commit sexual acts that previously were prohibited by criminal law (California Penal Code, 1975). Over 800,000 legal abortions were reported performed in 1975 (U.S. Department of Health, Education and Welfare, 1978).

The figures represent a trend in American public policy and law. For the past twenty years, there has been a shift toward the reduction of the scope of the substantive criminal law, particularly in the area of so-called "victimless" crimes.

A considerable amount of research has shown that attempts by the state to legislate morality in the use of drugs, sexual relations, gambling, pornography—the classic vices—have

AUTHORS' NOTE: *This paper is one result of support from the National Science Foundation's Law and Social Science Division, Grant No. SOC 74-13683.*

proved inconsistent, repressive, and ineffective. Several states have acted in the past ten years to remove criminal penalties or reduce them considerably for these crimes without victims, and the federal government supports substantially liberalized laws in at least one instance—the case of marijuana.

It is conceivable that in the next ten years marijuana will be virtually decriminalized in this country, that casino gambling will extend to half a dozen states—within driving distance of the majority of Americans—and that experiments with the decriminalization of heroin, cocaine, and prostitution will be proposed in several jurisdictions, and even adopted in a few. We are progressing from an era of the attempted prohibition of social deviance—really sin and criminality—to a more permissive era of legalization.

When we move, however, from concepts like sin and its legal counterpart, vice, to concepts like decriminalization and legalization, we solve some problems, but create new ones. In fact, we find ourselves shifting from the relative conceptual simplicity of criminal prohibition to the subtlety and complexity of administrative regulation. Agencies of decriminalization are devised by law-making bodies to replace earlier models of morality enforcement.

This area—the *regulation* of morality—should be an important and enduring concern for criminologists and sociologists of law in the coming years. Concomitantly, the emergent concern in the field of social deviance will no longer be with the issue of whether vices should be legalized, but with the question of appropriate forms, accompanying constraints, and collateral effects of legalization models.

VICTIMLESS CRIME

Part of the problem in formulating an adequate theory of decriminalization is the fuzziness of the concept "victimless crime," The activities encompassed by the concept vary greatly in whether they can be considered as merely socially opprobrious or truly and seriously harmful. The other part derives from the inconsistency of our society in legislating morality. Bedau (in Schur and Bedau, 1974: 100-101) asks:

> Why, for example, do we allow persons to gamble with their money, so long as they spend it on some risky ventures (the stock market), but prohibit them if they wish to spend it on others (offtrack betting, the numbers pool)? Why do we license the sale of some personal services (escort services, massage parlors) and not others ("massage parlors," prostitution)? Why do we allow some demonstrably harmful substances to be sold without prescription and merely tax them (tobacco, alcohol) whereas some others (marijuana, cocaine) are unavailable over the counter at all?

Bedau concludes that the explanation is not logical or moral, but *ideological* and *historical*. That conclusion is supported by the work of Duster (1970), Becker (1963), and Schur (1965), among others, in its application to the criminalization question.

The time is ripe for studies of these legal changes. Moreover, as Taylor, Walton, and Young (1974: 274) suggest, there is a great need for research into the political economy of social control:

> For the moment it is sufficient to assert that one of the important formal requirements of a fully social theory of deviance, that is almost totally absent in existing literature, is an effective model of the political and economic imperatives that underpin on the one hand the "lay ideologies" and on the other the "crusades" and initiatives that emerge periodically either to control the amount and level of deviance or else (as in the cases of prohibition, certain homosexual activity, and, most recently, certain "crimes without victims") to remove certain behaviors from the category of "illegal" behaviors. We are lacking a *political economy of social reaction.*

Similarly, Packer (1968: 354) observes that regulated vice is an "untapped field for students of social control." Skolnick (1978) recently completed a participant observation study of the agency which regulates casino gambling in Nevada. We hope that this proves to be a step in the direction of understanding the actual consequences and limits of decriminalization processes. Such an investigation, it turns out, is in fact a study of the political economy of societal reaction to deviance.

REGULATION

Scholars from the mid-nineteenth century on have debated two persistent themes relating to so-called vice. (1) Should criminal law be employed to enjoin conduct that some find pleasurable and others think repugnant? (2) Should governmental authority to regulate certain forms of enterprise be limited? When vices are decriminalized and subjected to regulation by administrative agencies, the two issues are joined.

As we shall later discuss, the law does not necessarily disappear in decriminalization. Most of the models presented, and certainly the great majority of those actually considered by law-making institutions, involve some role for the state. When regulation occurs, as Freund (1933) points out, the legislative prohibition may be lifted, but the government does not retreat. If anything, regulation may offer a purer case of "control" than prohibition. For example, under prohibition the law did not actually control the use of alcohol, marijuana, and narcotics and may have given rise to greater use. This phenomenon, which might be called "jurogenesis," is akin to the "iatrogenesis" of medicine—the precipitation of a physical disorder by the diagnosis or treatment of a physician or surgeon.

Thus, as Duster (1970) observes, the act of prohibition itself—the model of criminalization—gave rise to resistance to the law, and increased the popularity of beverage alcohol. By cutting off the legal supply to all classes, he argues, and making violation of the law the only alternative to those middle class persons who wanted to drink, the Volstead Act caused flagrant violations of the law, and produced the conditions for a public reappraisal of the moral status of alcohol consumption.

Similarly, when the. public came to view disrespectable elements as the primary indulgers—as in the case of heroin and morphine—the behavior came to be viewed as deviant and immoral. Thus, the acceptability of certain behavior tends to vary positively with the social position of users, and vice versa (National Commission, 1931).

When decriminalization is entertained, new issues arise around the moral quality of the formerly deviant activity. Is it still to be considered "evil conduct" even though legal? A variety of publics must reconsider and negotiate their acceptability of it. These include, in addition to potential consumers, governmental bodies ranging from legislators to police agencies. But other institutions may be involved as well. Capital-generating institutions like banks, insurance companies, stock exchanges, and pension funds must reconsider investment opportunities, when the activity prompts a capital intensive industry like the casino gambling business. Assuming that brothels were to be made legal—and indisputably profitable—should a conventional institutional lender employ strictly capitalistic criteria of potential profitability in deciding to finance? Thus, decriminalization generates issues of political and *moral* economy.

TRANSFORMATION

Although the political and moral economy of vice is scarcely of novel concern, its emergence in a legal setting in the past twenty years adds a new dimension. Since powerful illegal economies are now built around the provision of illicit goods and services, there may be some opposition to legalization from the very persons whose activities would be decriminalized. As Packer (1968: 354) notes, this is a fascinating research question:

> If a carefully devised and well-financed campaign were mounted in some state to secure sweeping measures of decriminalization for gambling that minimized the chances for underworld takeover, it would be interesting to study the sources of opposition. Much of it, predictably, would come from highly moralistic quarters. The point of special interest is this: which side would the underworld be on?

Recently, as the New York State legislature considered legalization of casino gambling, open opposition derived from an unusual combination of lobbyfellows—church groups, sheriffs, and horseracing interests (New York Times, 1978).

Thus, whatever the purpose in legalizing, the transformation from the criminal to the legal may not lack paradox. Usually, legalization connotes a less moralistic and rigid attitude toward the activity in question. For instance, proponents of marijuana legalization are generally regarded as liberals, their opponents as conservatives. But if legalization of marijuana were to occur, the alcohol and casino gambling model would suggest that strong bureaucratic controls would be applied to dealing in marijuana, whereas the present illegal traffic in marijuana actually constitutes the freest of enterprise, entirely unconstrained by controls deplored by doctrinaire conservatives.

MODELS

Various drugs other than marijuana, cocaine, and heroin are already under control in this country, with considerably less reliance upon the criminal law. Insurance companies, which are similar in many ways to numbers games, are subject to regulatory constraints. There are parallels all along the way. These comparisons are valuable, for it may be from existing control structures and theories that models of decriminalization will be drawn. "We may have to select among a set of already existing legal models," Kaplan (1971: 313) explains, "for the control of substances, to modify one of these, or perhaps to create a whole new type of legal treatment."

The reasons for decriminalization vary. The most important reason to repeal the prohibition of marijuana, Kaplan (1971: 312) writes, "is not that the drug is good but that the costs of criminalization are out of proportion to the benefits of this policy." Bonnie and Whitebread (1974: 301) conclude in their study of the criminalization of marijuana that the most compelling reason for modification is the disastrous impact upon the law as an institution:

> The utility or propriety of a criminal law is not measured in votes but in shared values. Price controls and other regulatory activities derive their legitimacy from the support of a majority, however transient; but outright criminal prohibitions, particularly those involving private behavior, derive their legitimacy from congruence with more enduring normative precepts.

Once these shared values are at variance with the law, the law must overextend itself to enforce their provisions.

Obviously, the range of possible alternatives to current policies is substantial and the issues pertaining to them complex and variable. Schur (Schur and Bedau, 1974: 44) explains:

> The problems posed by state-organized gambling are different from those presented by licensed prostitution; those involved in a scheme for government regulation of marijuana distri-

bution undoubtedly differ from those present in programs of methadone or heroin-maintenance for opiate addicts.

An adequate theory needs to embrace these very different control problems.

The commercial potential and other economic aspects—especially the importance of capital to the activity—determine the appropriateness of the model of legalization. Some vices enjoy more commercial potential than others. One can scarcely imagine how to commercialize homosexuality. Homosexual prostitution exists, of course, but so does heterosexual prostitution. It is the sale of sex, regardless of the gender of the parties, that yields profit. While alcoholic beverages, tobacco, marijuana, and cocaine—as well as various sorts of gambling—lend themselves easily to an industrywide organization, prostitution does not, despite its commercial potential. In summary, we suggest that, in thinking about decriminalization, at least six models should be considered: nullification, a commodity regulation model, a commercial service model, a vice model, a medical model, and a licensing model.

Nullification. Under this model, the law withdraws entirely. While this may not resemble a rational alternative to the treatment of an activity which was previously a crime, it theoretically remains a possiblity. Sexual relations between consenting adults exemplifies this model. What Packer (1968: 366) suggests is that often our alternative need not be specified:

> The real alternative in many cases will turn out to be doing nothing (as a matter of legal compulsion), or at any rate doing less. Distasteful as that alternative may sometimes seem, we need to press the inquiry whether it is not preferable to doing what we are now doing.

A commodity model. Under a commodity model, a substance, such as marijuana, would be treated like a plant or

vegetable. Thus, one could buy seed packets at the neighborhood gardening store, plant them in the backyard, cure the
leaves, and use the marijuana freely. It could also be grown
commercially in fields, and sold as a vegetable in vegetable
stores.

Under this model, the law would largely withdraw, and only
enforce minimal guarantees of quality and purity. Except for
that, the substance would be allowed to be freely produced,
sold, and advertised.

Without getting ahead of our argument, suffice it to say
that the commodity model is of limited applicability. It is
inadequate in most cases because it lacks a necessary presumption: that society no longer wishes to deter use of the
formerly illegal substances. Kaplan (1971: 314) and other
advocates of decriminalization, for example, argue that marijuana is not to be promoted in the same manner as avocados:

> although the costs of using the criminal law to outlaw these
> "socially approved" drugs obviously outweigh the benefits
> of criminalizing them, this does not mean that society has no
> strong interest in minimizing the abuse of these drugs.

While lawmakers may decide that an activity such as prostitution is not sufficiently harmful to the social and moral
environment of a community to require the present penalties,
they may not consider the activity healthy enough to be
encouraged.

A commercial service model. Prostitution has been increasingly projected as a candidate for legalization, since it
usually involves consenting sex between adults. But prostitution also implies consenting *payment.* It provides a commercial as well as a sexual service. Why should sexual services
be exempted from regulation when other consenting commercial activities are regulated?

For example, when one person invites another home for a
meal, the state ordinarily evidences no interest in the activity.

But when the meal is available to the general public provided one can pay, when a private kitchen is transformed into a public restaurant, other considerations emerge.

Those selling food are regulated in a variety of ways. A restaurant may not operate in an area zoned solely for residences. A street vendor must normally obtain a permit before being allowed to sell peanuts, pretzels, or hot dogs. In addition, those who sell food—in contrast to those who give it to friends—are normally regulated for cleanliness. The private kitchen can be unwashed. But when the public is charged a price for the privilege of eating, consumer protection norms formalized into law propel the state into an obligation to inquire whether the kitchen is clean. Although it does not follow as day from night, ordinarily legalization of commercial services provokes regulation.

A vice model. To date, this has been the most acceptable model for decriminalization, probably because it conforms most closely to the criminalization model. Under this solution, the sale and manufacture of something like marijuana is heavily penalized, while no criminal penalties attend to the use or possession of small amounts of cannabis. In other words, selling or trafficking in marijuana remains criminal, but the mere user is freed completely from any threat of criminal punishment. This is the model now used in handling most gambling, abortion, and prostitution cases—the seller is liable but the customer is guilty of no criminal offense. It is the plan recommended by the National Commission on Marijuana and Drug Abuse.

The model is obviously not rational. By allowing personal use while heavily prohibiting sale and manufacture, it recapitulates all of the problems of the alcohol prohibition model. As long as we criminalize sellers and drive them underground, we cannot exercise the necessary controls on either the quality or kinds of drugs they sell. In addition, illegal selling will continue to be the entry into a ready distribution market for many people.

The politics of legalization dictate such mixed and confused models. Even though California did pass liberalized laws for marijuana possession, an Assembly bill to reduce penalties for personal cultivation was handily defeated in January of 1978 (San Francisco Chronicle, 1978). Legislators who had been persuaded to support a liberalized possession law were not convinced that similar handling of small scale cultivation would not encourage the use of marijuana. This despite a report by the California State Office of Narcotics and Drug Abuse (1977: 11) which concluded that "the reduction in penalties for possession of marijuana for personal use does not appear to have been a major factor in people's decision to use or not to use the drug." The National Organization for the Reform of Marijuana Laws had hoped for this change, and now it appears that—despite the Carter administration's support for liberalized laws—the model most likely to be employed in the case of marijuana is the vice model.

We must conclude that here, as in many other areas of the law, legal reform is not as much a result of rational analysis so much as it reflects legislative innovation grafted onto a history of legal rules and social symbols. The definitional and political character of social problems is paramount. Such considerations similarly affect physicians' opinions of the medical potential of drugs. Thus, Grinspoon (1977: 399) writes:

> When marijuana was regarded as the drug of blacks, Mexican Americans and bohemians, doctors were ready to go along with the Federal Bureau of Narcotics, ignore its medical uses, and urge prohibition. . . . Now that marijuana has become so popular among middle-class youth, we are willing to investigate its therapeutic value seriously.

A medical model. This model, which is often proposed as an alternative to present narcotic policies, would—unlike the vice model—involve a drastic change from the present law. Under this plan, marijuana, heroin, or cocaine would be defined as sedatives or stimulants and be sold like similar drugs, under a doctor's prescription. Conclusions from the British experience with heroin under such a method portray a complex system, with new problems generated by the solution. Still, the prevention of secondary crime is a compelling argument for the medical treatment of heroin addiction.

Applying this model to something like marijuana exposes some of the difficulties. While it is theoretically promising, it is practically problematic. Prohibition, after all, unsuccessfully applied the medical model to alcohol.

Presumably, a large number of marijuana users would be able to convince their doctors that they needed the substance because it helps them relax from everyday stress and strain. Herein lies the problem. Fundamentally, marijuana, like alcohol, tobacco, and coffee, is a recreational drug. While many physicians may favor some sort of decriminalization, they would, Kaplan (1971: 332) argues, not really be prescribing out of a concern for the patient's health, but in order to lessen the costs to patients and society of the application of sanctions for the violation of the criminal law. It is unlikely that the medical profession could be convinced that the prescription of marijuana was one of its crucial functions.

A licensing model. Licensing merges the traditional social task of character assessment with procedural formalities of legal governance. Yet, given the broad discretion—and variation—in licensing, licensing boards and processes seem to present the most developed form of modern governmental bureaucracy.

Licensing is intimately related to social purpose, express or implied—and more than one is quite possible. Friedman (1965: 496), for example, distinguishes between "hostile" and "friendly" licensing. To illustrate, he cites, on the one hand, peddlers' licenses in Wisconsin, intended to diminish the competition to local businesses of transients, and, on the other, dentists' licenses, where the profession was delegated the authority to pretty much govern itself.

Whoever licenses, the process is potentially exclusionary. Under licensing, the question is what criteria come to be employed, other than loose, vague, and general ones like "good character." Under licensing, the legalization of vice is seen at its most problematic: a battery of questions for rule makers and rule enforcers arises. For example, what standards should be employed to decide who is to be allowed to practice the legalized activity? Should applicants be excluded because of a prior occupational history when the activity was illegal? Does it matter what sort of history they have? Is it relevant to ask whether they were part of organized crime? If so, how is organized crime to be defined?

Those who did hold positions in prior illegal enterprises were often involved in corrupting government officials. How is it possible to maintain honesty in contemporary governmental control operations when an industry contains operators who have probably, if not demonstrably, corrupted public officials in the past? What standards should be employed for selecting controllers and for assessing their present work? What sort of relationship should obtain between them and contemporary political authorities?

The licensing model of decriminalization, as entailed in most of the gambling experiments, generates these questions. A vice model, such as those variations employed in the decriminalization of marijuana, does, but less so. Both examples are important to theories and research strategies for analyzing decriminalization. Both pose a central question of this area of social deviance: when a deviant social activity, formerly outlawed because it was regarded as immoral, becomes legal, however restricted, does it lose its opprobrium through legalization? Is the ill-repute of the activity reduced by its association with legal authorities who have declared it to be within the realm of acceptable conduct? Or does the moral obloquy attaching to the activity discredit the legalizers?

The movement to license a formerly deviant activity thus carries in its wake two associated sets of problems: (1) how to develop and organize legal institutions to assess, define, and manage the economics of an ill-reputed activity through the use of state power, and (2) how to insulate the controllers from the stigma associated with the activity.

This is further complicated by the social purpose of decriminalization and licensing. Nevada licenses casino gambling primarily to produce income for the state, which takes 5½ percent of gross gaming revenue. New Jersey has introduced casino gambling primarily to renew the popularity of a down-at-the-heels resort. Great Britain, by contrast, views gambling as a social problem, better dealt with through regulation than criminalization. Unlike Nevada and New Jersey, the British explicitly seek to regulate so as *not* to stimulate demand for gambling. Whether they succeed is another question.

In any event, licensing is clearly the most popular and most complex of the decriminalization models, offering a fascinating terrain for research on the legal process and the future of social deviance.

CONCLUSION

We do not know which of the above models will be appropriate in any given instance, but we are confident that any experimentation will have to be made along the lines of one or more of them. We are also confident that, as new models are developed, new problems will arise that may well suggest a kind of dialectical return to the earlier questions in the field of deviance. These will derive from what might be called the *collateral* problems of legalization.

For example, assume a society comes to accept the idea that homosexual relations between consenting adults is no longer "deviant conduct," to be punished by criminal law. Collateral problems arise such as whether homosexuals will be allowed to enter "sanctified institutions" such as marriage, or be allowed to adopt children—or even to teach them.

Should prostitution be decriminalized, what should society's position be on whether pimping and pandering should remain criminal activities? Or, as in West Germany, will prostitutes prefer to avoid mandatory licensing, fearing the residual stigmatization? A society legalizes off-track betting. Will an illegal gambling culture reemerge in response to a system of regulation that exacts too much in the way of taxes?

Just as there are different political, economic, and historical bases for the stigma attached to certain activities—addicts created by medical treatment are perceived differently than those produced by a drug subculture—the processes of legalization will encounter a wide variety of novel problems. Distinctions will also need to be drawn between private morality —e.g., the morality of a friendly crapshoot—versus public morality—e.g., the use of legal casino gambling to help resolve the fiscal crisis of the state.

The emergent concerns of the fields of criminology and social deviance will no longer be with the traditional "victimless crime" focus—i.e., whether vice should be legalized—but with the structural features, accompanying constraints, and collateral effects of legalization models.

REFERENCES

BECKER, H. (1963) Outsiders: Studies in the Sociology of Deviance. New York: Free Press.
BONNIE, R. and C. WHITEBREAD (1974) The Marihuana Conviction. Charlottesville: Univ. Press of Virginia.
BROWNELL, G. (1977) "Marijuana: fertilizing the liberal trend." Los Angeles Times (November 21).

California Penal Code (1975) Sections 220, 269, 286, 287, 288, 290.

California State Office of Narcotics and Drug Abuse (1977) "A first report of the impact of California's new marijuana law (SB 95)."

Commission on the Review of the National Policy Toward Gambling (1976) Gambling in America. Washington, DC: Government Printing Office.

DUSTER, T. (1970) The Legislation of Morality. New York: Free Press.

FREUND, E. (1933) "Licensing," pp. 447-450, Vol. IX, Encyclopaedia of Social Sciences. New York: Macmillan.

FRIEDMAN, L. (1965) "Freedom of contract and occupational licensing 1890-1910: a legal and social study." Calif. Law Rev. 53: 487-534.

GRINSPOON, L. (1977) Marihuana Reconsidered. Cambridge, MA: Harvard Univ. Press.

KAPLAN, J. (1971) Marijuana: The New Prohibition. New York: Meridian.

National Commission on Law Observance and Enforcement (1931) "Report on the enforcement of the Prohibition laws of the United States." H.R. Doc. No. 722, 71st Cong., 3d Sess.

New York Times (1978) February 26.

PACKER, H. (1968) The Limits of the Criminal Sanction. Stanford, CA: Stanford Univ. Press.

San Francisco Chronicle (1978) January 31.

SCHUR, E. (1965) Crimes Without Victims. Englewood Cliffs, NJ: Prentice-Hall.

——— and H. A. BEDAU (1974) Victimless Crimes: Two Sides of a Controversy. Englewood Cliffs, NJ: Prentice-Hall.

SKOLNICK, J. (1978) House of Cards: Legalization and Control of Casino Gambling. Boston: Little, Brown.

TAYLOR, I., P. WALTON, and J. YOUNG (1974) The New Criminology. New York: Harper Torchbooks.

U.S. Department of Health, Education and Welfare (1978) "Abortion surveillance report." Atlanta: Center for Disease Control.

U.S. Treasury Department (1978) "Alcohol, tobacco, and firearms summary statistics." Washington, DC: Bureau of Alcohol, Tobacco, and Firearms.

7

THE COUNTERPRODUCTIVITY OF
CONSERVATIVE THINKING ABOUT CRIME

DANIEL GLASER
University of Southern California

t he patterns of thought about crime that are usually labeled "conservative" are motivated by a desire to reduce lawbreaking, but they produce policies that increase crime. Such unanticipated effects occur at every level of the criminal justice system, from police through courts to corrections. Nonetheless, commentators on the issues discussed here cannot be neatly categorized, for some of the ideas appropriately labeled "conservative" often are espoused by persons generally called "liberal."

CONCEPTIONS OF POLICE ROLES

The conservative emphasis in policing is on "law and order," or what Packer (1968) called the "crime control" model of criminal justice administration. It views the police primarily as warriors in combat with criminals (although this has never been what most police usually do). When this main thrust of conservative leadership dominates police policy, it has deleterious effects on the community, the criminal justice system, and the crime rates.

There is little that the police can do to reduce quickly and clearly the rates of FBI "Index Crimes" (murder, aggravated assault, rape, robbery, burglary, larceny, and auto theft) that are generally used in assessing a community's conformity to the law. As Manning (1974, 1977) brilliantly shows, about all that police can do to dramatize their proficiency as warriors against crime is (1) to combat Index Crimes by tactics that impair the rest of the criminal justice system and mask offense rates, and (2) to concentrate on other types of law violations, such as narcotics and prostitution, which usually do not generate complainants but may be exposed by aggressive search and by entrapment.

Law enforcement that is oriented to public and political relationships concentrates on making conspicuous arrests, but is indifferent to its rate of achieving convictions. Typically, while conservative police officials blame the courts for failures to convict or for reductions of charges and mild sentences, they never compile statistics that could relate variations in police procedure to prospects of successful prosecution. Indeed, such figures could embarrass the police since most felony charges that arresting officers make are dropped by state or district attorneys as unprosecutable. Law enforcement agencies prefer to focus on their clearance rate. This is the percentage of crimes that they believe they investigated adequately, and does not depend upon their ability to convince a court that they are correct in this judgment.

Some conservative police agencies may go further and markedly distort their crime statistics by failing to record some offenses reported to them that they have little prospect of clearing. Therefore, police forces are said to vary in their rates of "unfounding" complaints to avoid counting these as "crimes known to the police" (Manning, 1977: 132). Cities also vary in the extent to which victims of crimes deem it worthwhile to report offenses to the police. One clue to the magnitude of these sources of error in our police-derived *Uniform Crime Reports* was provided by the federal surveys on victimization. They showed that citizens claimed to have suffered five times as many Index Crimes as were reported by a highly politicized police force in Philadelphia, but only about twice as many as the police reported in New York City, where law enforcement has been less obsessed with conservative showmanship (Glaser, 1978: 58-70).

The leading spokesmen for conservative attitudes on policing (especially chiefs of large city forces who aspired to elective office), decried the victim surveys. Apparently sensitive to such pressures, the Department of Justice has usually kept the victim-survey data not readily comparable to the FBI figures. In 1977 it suspended these surveys temporarily; let us hope that it is working to improve them as our one independent check on police-reported offense trends, and on crime-victims' attitudes toward the police.

In trying to clear crimes for which they have no clues, or as a crime-prevention measure, some overeager warriors against lawbreaking harass large numbers of persons known or alleged to have committed offenses in the past. They frequently detain them for questioning, and threaten or arrest them with little justification. Such "busywork" tactics violate the spirit and often the letter of the Bill of Rights, contribute little to the solution of puzzling crimes, and cause many former offenders trying to "go straight" to lose jobs and be stigmatized again, thus often fostering recidivism.

These expressions of conservative police thought tend to be applied predominantly to one age group, while quite contrasting conduct is directed to other age groups, and thus their net effects widen the generation gap. Specifically, police "community relations" programs in many neighborhoods are concerned mostly with befriending the older population and sometimes the primary school children, but police actions with junior high and high school students in the same areas consist too exclusively of "hassling" by sidewalk interrogation, threat, and arrest. Such conflict with adolescents and young adults is related to conservative policies on drug law enforcement, to be discussed later.

Originally, police in British and American cities were watchmen. They were not always expected to catch criminals, but were at least to "give hue and cry," so that other citizens could take up the chase. Their responsibility was to give or procure aid in any emergency, whether criminal, medical, fire, or other. Such a watch corps, that today can be readily reached by telephone and radio, is more important than ever now that the relatives and friends of most persons are widely dispersed, even when in the same metropolitan area. The police are the only agency everywhere available 24 hours a day, seven days a week, to give many kinds of immediate aid and to summon other kinds. But this is not the function that police stress when they become huge bureaucracies with highly centralized control under conservative leaders who try to portray themselves primarily as warrior chiefs in a battle against evil.

Research has shown that metropolitan law enforcement is more cost-effective and creates in the public a greater sense of being protected from crime when police are decentralized (Ostrom et al., 1973), so that they can be better acquainted with residents of their district and can be known by them. A crucial resource that can always be cultivated more by the police is the universal norm of reciprocity (Gouldner, 1960), whereby persons who believe that they have been well-treated feel obligated to repay the favor. This resource is most clearly recognized and exploited by what Wilson (1968) called the "service" style of policing; it stresses friendliness to residents, provision of a large variety of assistance, quick response, good manners, and making a favorable impression. If (1) police organization is decentralized, so that each fairly autonomous unit is assigned regularly to as small a territory as is practical, and if (2) officers strive for a service rather than a warrior style, more people will regard them favorably, cooperate with them, and feel safer from crime. Statistics on all services rendered would be helpful in their public relations. But community attitudes also depend upon the types of offenses on which law enforcement efforts are concentrated.

THE POLICE
AND NONCOMPLAINANT CRIMES

There has never been a clear net benefit to society from the second major focus of conservative police, their advocacy and enforcement of laws that completely prohibit widespread activities which all participants desire and can easily hide, such as prostitution or the use of alcohol or other drugs. We should have learned from frustration with the Eighteenth Amendment, and from decades of failure with all levels of penalty for commercial sex and for drug abuse, that if the criminal justice system seeks to suppress totally any widespread behavior in which none of those involved consider themselves victimized, it (1) alienates much of the otherwise law-abiding public, and (2) becomes unfair or currupt. Now that the Gallup Polls show that a majority of our population 18 to 30 years old have used marijuana, it is obvious that the persons offended by enforcement of laws against this substance are an appreciable and growing number. If it is answered that these laws are not extensively enforced, the unfairness and potential corruption are also obvious.

The Index offenses are acts that almost everyone considers criminal, and police investigating them are usually reacting to complaints from victims or their families. Contrastingly, for those types of crimes that rarely are reported to the police, law enforcement efforts depend mainly upon paid informants, entrapment, and illegal search. The disrespect for the police generated by the questionable legality of such tactics, plus the gaps in public support of the laws against practices that many persons accept (or at least tolerate in others if done in private), alienate much of the citizenry. Thus, police enforcement of laws against nonpredatory acts may impede public cooperation in the enforcement of laws against more clearly victimizing offenses, such as theft and assault.

When the demand for illegal goods or services is highly inelastic, police efforts to enforce prohibitions only affect the visibility of these offenses, never their prevalence for long. Blockage of some sources of supply soon increases the profit, hence the enterprise, in others (including, for example, sales of substitute drugs often more dangerous than those previously used). Furthermore, because efforts to prohibit sales of a highly addictive substance, such as heroin, make the price so high that most addicts must commit crimes to procure funds to purchase it, the principal effect of more enforcement of current laws banning such drugs is to increase the volume of property crimes, for more of these offenses are then perpetrated by addicts (Fujii, 1975; Votey and Phillips, 1976).

American and British experience in trying to control alcohol and opiates during the past half-century clearly demonstrates that the personal suffering from using such drugs and the social costs from their promoting professional and organized crime are lessened when the government tries only to regulate their distribution rather than to prohibit them. All that the criminal justice system can accomplish with much success in combating substance abuse, as well as in opposing commercial sex, is to minimize their visibility and profit, and this is best done with licensing laws having these objectives. Our main resources for cutting the prevalence and social costs of private vices are not the criminal justice system, but consist of (1) public-health education, and (2) economic and sociocultural conditions and public recreational facilities that maximize opportunities for satisfaction in legal alternative activities.

ADJUDICATION

The conservative perspective in our courts is articulated whenever prosecutors and judges run for elective office of any type. Its goals are high conviction rates and mandatory sentences. Its effects, however, are grossly capricious convictions, haphazard sentences, and only an illusion of an adversary system.

So great is the concern of politically ambitious prosecutors with appealing to conservative thinking about crime among the electorate that they feel obliged to have well over 90% conviction rate, lest they be accused of slackness in the "war against crime." To achieve such a rate, they must usually decline to prosecute most of the charges that police make, and must reduce the severity of many of the remainder. If case negotiation were done by a systematic procedure, well-monitored to assure its conformity with principles of justice, it might be tolerable. The procedure, however, is typically one of casual and private interaction between junior staff of the prosecution office and either public or private defense lawyers. Its outcome closely reflects the justice-irrelevant pressures in their offices to clear cases from their workloads at that particular moment, the private lawyer's desire to squeeze retainers out of the families of clients, and whatever bias any of the attorneys may have for or against particular types of defendants (Sudnow, 1965; Newman, 1966, 1974; Blumberg, 1966; Alschuler, 1968, 1975; Rosett and Cressey, 1976; Bernstein et al., 1977a, 1977b; Stanko, 1977; Hagan et al., 1978).

These features of our adjudication processes have the following consequences.

1. A sham is made of the claim in our courts that "a defendant is considered innocent until proved guilty," since—in at least three-fourths of the cases—pretrial negotiation is conducted with both sides assuming the guilt of the accused but bargaining over what the offense should be called or on the sentence that the prosecution will recommend.

2. Mandatory or unusually severe sentencing laws are routinely evaded, especially in busy urban courts; their only effect is to give the prosecution an additional edge in bargaining, so that the charge carrying a maximum penalty can be waived in exchange for a plea of guilty on something else. Thus, since California reinstated capital punishment (inevita-

bly the most capricious sentence, as Black, 1974, shows), only about 10% of hearings to impose capital punishment following convictions for first degree murder in Los Angeles County result in death penalty sentences, as compared with 50% in less urban California counties, where there is less plea bargaining (Multhaup, 1976). Similarly, a desire to make sentences more predictable leads conservatives and some liberals (e.g., Morris, 1974; van den Haag, 1975; von Hirsch, 1976) to endorse new definite-sentencing laws (such as those of California); yet charge bargaining makes these laws relatively ineffective, except that if potential severity of penalty is increased, so also is actual variability (and probably, in some cases, pleading to a lesser charge rather than risking trial on a serious charge, even though innocent of all charges).

3. The safeguards against improper evidence or argument that distinguish our trial procedures usually become irrelevant because about 90% of cases do not go to trial, and case negotiation occurs in private—often by telephone—and thus not subject to procedural objection or review.

4. The Sixth Amendment's guarantee of a speedy trial for the accused and the court restriction on prosecution delay generally are irrelevant, since it is the defense that usually seeks delay; time is to its advantage in plea bargaining and in collecting fees from relatives of the defendant or from a defendant out on bail.

5. Concern with presentence reports or with judicial wisdom in sentencing often is largely irrelevant because the sentencing options are greatly diminished by charge or sentence bargaining.

Of course, the conditions in our courts indicated above do not result entirely from conservative thinking about crime, but they are aggravated by conservatives' demands that courts convict virtually all arrestees and impose uniformly severe sentences. The most prominent proposal to alleviate those conditions sparked controversy between Chief Justice Burger and the American Bar Association in 1978. Apparently he sought to have trial lawyers screened in order to reduce rhetoric, motions, and requests for continuances that do not help the court arrive at truth but instead are plea bargaining tactics intended to impede case resolution (such antics of attorneys have long been restricted in Britain through rigid licensing and monitoring of barristers). Less drastic reforms, some already adopted in the federal courts, require that all plea bargain be a matter of public record, and make any clear violation of their terms a basis for appeal. More effective, perhaps, would be the domination of pretrial investigating and bargaining by an active, powerful, adequately pretested and closely monitored career judge, similar to the examining magistrate of Continental European courts. As on the Continent, whenever the judge's examination results in charges that are very serious, an adversary procedure would follow, even with a guilty plea (since it would have to be corroborated by other evidence). Also, prosecutors should be disciplined civil servants and not elected or politically appointed. Probably we can improve on the adjudication procedures of any single European country if we strive for what is best from all systems; to achieve this, however, requires more imagination and willingness to experiment than our lawyer-dominated legislatures are likely to permit.

CORRECTIONS

The epitome of conservative thinking on corrections, as already indicated, is the advocacy of more capital and other severe punishment. Increasingly shared with liberals are the conservatives' opposition to parole and their glib assertions that correctional programs "never rehabilitate." They also oppose probation for any serious charges unless it begins with a period of incarceration (Wilson, 1975: 180). All of these policies, it will be argued, expand our crime rates.

Capital punishment is likely to be the most inconsistently applied penalty in the United States because, as our discussion of the courts pointed out, it has the greatest potential for manipulation in plea bargaining. Also, the claim that it deters homicide more than do alternative penalties of long imprisonment may well be the opposite of statistically demonstrable fact. There was a direct correlation between use of the death penalty and homicide rates in 1933-1963, when both generally declined, and an inverse relationship for a dozen years thereafter, when the homicide rate rose while the executions continued to decline. Ehrlich (1975) points out that murder rates in the 1930s were highly correlated with unemployment and in the 1960s with the percentage of the population aged 14 through 24. He claims to show a close relationship between the death penalty and murder rates by employing (1) a complex multivariate analysis that purports to subtract the influence of other variables on the homicide rate, and (2) a logarithmic transformation that gives much greater weight to each annual decline in executions when they approached zero during the 1960s (while homicides were rising) than to the much greater decline in executions during 1930-1960 (when homicides generally were declining also). The rise in homicides during the 1960s was probably related to race relations trends in our country during this riotous decade that Ehrlich's statistics do not take into account (see Glaser, 1978: 228-232). Furthermore, if one bears in mind that executions in the United States totaled less than 2% of homicides before 1953 and less than 1% thereafter, Ehrlich's claim that the death penalty greatly affects our homicide rates seems questionable from the outset, and others have shown that different types of reasonable statistical procedures would yield conclusions quite opposite to his (Bowers and Price, 1975; Zeisel, 1977; Forst, 1977). Of more profound importance, perhaps, is the highly suggestive evidence that either use or legislative endorsement of capital punishment fosters indifference toward murder, since these policies are associated with both the highest murder rates and the shortest prison terms for murder (all of the foregoing argument and evidence are elaborated in Glaser, 1977a).

Opposition to parole is based largely on the assumption that parole boards determine release dates primarily by lay psychology in predicting dangerousness, and that this cannot be done with greater accuracy by them than by the legislature in prescribing mandatory terms for each type of offense or by judges in exercising whatever discretion in sentencing the law grants them. From having worked several years for both liberal and conservative parole boards in Illinois during the early 1950s, and in case-decision simulations, in small groups for a few days with each of a majority of parole board members in the United States during twelve of the one-week National Parole Institute's meetings during the early 1960s, I can assert with much confidence that the first concern of most parole boards with the vast majority of their cases is to reduce the disparity of penalties imposed by the courts. In examining a case file they first look at the description of the offense, to judge whether the length of sentence is proportional to the gravity of the actual crime, and they then assess how well the penalty takes into account the prior criminal record.

Most parole boards probably could do a much better job of reducing the variability of court penalties. Many boards are hasty and arbitrary. They sometimes impose long confinement for petty misconduct in prison or on parole, they frequently express personal prejudices or rely upon questionable evidence, and they certainly torment prisoners by keeping them uninformed about the duration of and the reasons for their further confinement. Nervertheless, parole could be improved instead of eliminated; until we get better court reform, including perhaps some other routine review of adjudication and sentencing (parole's main function), its preservation as one of the checks and balances in our system may be desirable. Changes in parole might include: (1) reducing the extreme range of discretion that some boards have, (2) depoliticizing them by making the members civil servants with highly relevant qualifications (as Wisconsin and Michigan have done), (3) expanding contract parole, whereby the release date is fixed soon after the prison term begins, because each inmate negotiates a mutual agreement with the board that specifies what objective acts and achievements will change the time of release from its maximum to an earlier date (as is now done in Minnesota, Wisconsin, Michigan, Maryland, and several other states; Leiberg and Parker, 1975; Gettinger, 1975).

The assertions that "nothing works" in rehabilitation programs cite primarily the survey by Lipton, Martinson, and Wilks (1975) that was not designed to test well-grounded theory on what forms of assistance reduce recidivism for what types of offenders (see Glaser, 1975, 1977b). Most of the evaluations that they covered neglect such criminologically relevant variables as (1) what the offenders objectively demonstrated that they learned or what tangible resources they received from a program (rather than whether they were merely exposed to it), (2) the social setting of a program, for example, whether it always handled large groups of offenders in a regimented manner, or separated them from persons of similar age and criminality to deal with them individually in a predominantly noncorrectional agency, (3) whether a treatment group that received appreciable economic or other assistance had recidivism rates that were differently related to the prior criminal and employment records of the offenders than were the rates in the control group. Yet despite the survey's pooling together the results from studies of extremely diverse conceptual and methodological quality, its glib conclusion is cited in argument for (1) constructing more large and remote bastilles, (2) restoring two coeducational federal prisons in California to one-sex occupancy, (3) assigning halfway-house residence in the city during the last three months of a prison term to white-collar criminals with adequate resources rather than to nonprofessional and nonaddicted ordinary offenders who are more likely to have their experiences changed favorably by ready access to shelter, food, and staff during their first few months out.

A surprising feature of conservative thinking about corrections is its frequent unwillingness to consider cost-benefit aspects of alternative programs. Thus, the principal architects of California's restoration of capital punishment opposed (unsuccessfully) a 1977 bill by which an inmate's work in prison creates eligibility for postrelease unemployment insurance. As I pointed out when proposing such a measure in the early 1960s (Glaser, 1964: 412-14), destitution among jobless parolees ineligible for unemployment compensation is highly associated with recidivism. Furthermore, controlled experiments in Maryland and California during the 1970s showed that modest weekly stipends to parolees when out of work reduce their violations sufficiently to be a net financial saving to the state (Reinarman and Miller, 1975; U.S. Department of Labor, 1977). These studies also indicate that such payments make the greatest reduction in recidivism rates for some types of offenders with poor prior records, as does release to a halfway house (Hall et al., 1966; Jeffery and Woolpert, 1974; Beha, 1977), but conservative correctional officials tend to reserve these forms of assistance for the best-risk offenders. The conservative alternative to imaginative investment in strategic assistance is to prevent the offenders from committing crimes by incapacitating them through imprisonment; Schrag (1977) estimates, however, that this costs an average of at least $35,000 for each crime that the prisoners would have committed if not confined, and they may still have higher recidivism rates when they finally are released than they would have if released earlier.

The conservative approach to corrections is also evident in the insistence that anyone given probation on a first conviction for a felony should initially be required to complete a term in jail. Often the first offender's public exposure by the arrest and conviction is in itself a traumatic penalty, but incarceration adds such crime-inducing experiences as loss of job or failure in school and an intimacy with more hardened offenders. If a first offender were likely to recidivate soon, the jail term that goes with probation usually would be only a brief incapacitation, but the actual probability of recidivism may well be increased by jailing. There certainly are other deterrents adequate for the lesser first felonies, notably fines, restitution, civic-duty obligations, and mandatory reporting for instruction or for mutual-aid programs. In many cases an imaginative judge and probation staff could impose these as probation conditions without also ordering the frequently criminogenic and no more deterrent experience of jail life.

SUMMARY AND CONCLUSION

Police efforts to dramatize a conception of their role solely as combatants with criminals result in criminogenic policing. Courts that insist too much on achieving perfect conviction records and consistently severe sentences make capricious case dispositions and erode our constitutional protections. Unless it is recognized that offenders are diverse, and that like all humans they change their conduct with intense alterations in their experiences, correctional programs will foster more recidivism and less reformation than they could. To approach maximum crime prevention we must especially avoid rigid dogmas; we should instead seek to test alternative policies to determine not just their outcomes, but the relative validity of alternative explanations for their outcomes. Wisdom for guiding our criminal justice system will come only from learning sound criminological principles through applying and testing relevant theory.

REFERENCES

ALSCHULER, A. W. (1975) "The defense attorney's role in plea bargaining." Yale Law J. 84: 1179-1314.
——— (1968) "The prosecutor's role in plea bargaining." Univ. of Chicago Law Rev. 36 (Fall): 50-112.
BEHA, J. A. II (1977) "Innovation at a county house of correction and its effects upon patterns of recidivism." Journal of Research in Crime and Delinquency 14 (January): 88-106.
BERNSTEIN, I. N., W. R. KELLY, and P. A. DOYLE (1977a) "Societal reaction to deviants: the case of criminal defendants." Amer. Soc. Rev. 42: 743-755.
BERNSTEIN, I. N., E. KICK, J. T. LEUNG, and B. SCHULZ (1977b) "Charge reduction: an intermediary stage in the process of labelling criminal defendants." Social Forces 56: 362-384.
BLACK, C. L., Jr. (1974) Capital Punishment: The Inevitability of Caprice and Mistake. New York: Norton.
BLUMBERG, A. S. (1966) "The practice of law as a confidence game." Law and Society Rev. 1 (June): 15-39.
BOWERS, W. J. and G. L. PRICE (1975) "The illusion of deterrence in Isaac Ehrlich's research on capital punishment." Yale Law J. 85: 187-208.

EHRLICH, I. (1975) "The deterrent effects of capital punishment: a question of life or death." Amer. Econ. Rev. 65: 397-417.

FORST, B. E. (1977) "The deterrent effect of capital punishment: a cross-state analysis in the 1960s." Minnesota Law Rev. 61: 743-767.

FUJII, E. T. (1975) "Heroin addiction and public policy." J. of Urban Economics 2: 181-198.

GETTINGER, S. (1975) "Parole contracts: a new way out." Corrections Magazine 2 (September/October): 3-8, 45-50.

GLASER, D. (1978) Crime in Our Changing Society. New York: Holt, Rinehart & Winston.

——— (1977a) "The realities of homicide versus the assumptions of economists in assessing capital punishment." J. of Behav. Economics 6: 243-268.

——— (1977b) "Concern with theory in correctional evaluation research." Crime and Delinquency 23: 173-179.

——— (1975) "Achieving better questions: a half century's progress in correctional research." Federal Probation 39 (September): 3-9.

——— (1964) The Effectiveness of a Prison and Parole System. Indianapolis: Bobbs-Merrill.

GOULDNER, A. W. (1960) "The norm of reciprocity." Amer. Soc. Rev. 25: 161-178.

HAGAN, J., J. HEWITT, and D. ALWIN (1978) "Ceremonial justice: crime and punishment in a loosely coupled system." Paper presented to Society for Study of Social Problems, San Francisco.

HALL, R. H., M. MILAZZO, and J. POSNER (1966) A Descriptive and Comparative Study of Recidivism in Prerelease Guidance Center Releasees. Washington, DC: U.S. Bureau of Prisons.

JEFFERY, R. and S. WOOLPERT (1974) "Work furlough as an alternative to incarceration: an assessment of its effects on recidivism and social cost." J. of Criminal Law and Criminology 65: 405-415.

LEIBERG, L. and W. PARKER (1975) "Mutual agreement programs with vouchers: an alternative for institutionalized female offenders." Amer. J. of Correction 37 (January/February): 10-13, 38.

LIPTON, D., R. MARTINSON, and J. WILKS (1975) The Effectiveness of Correctional Treatment: A Survey of Treatment Evaluation Studies. New York: Praeger.

MANNING, P. K. (1977) The Social Organization of Policing. Cambridge, MA: MIT Press.

——— (1974) "Dramatic aspects of policing: selected propositions." Sociolgy and Social Research 59 (October): 21-29.

MORRIS, N. (1974) The Future of Imprisonment. Chicago: Univ. of Chicago Press.

MULTHAUP, E. (1976) Special compilation from 12 counties, in defense testimony. People v. Wayne Frederick Barnes. Calif. Sup. Ct., Los Angeles, Dept. 111, Case A316381.

NEWMAN, D. J. (1974) "Role and process in the criminal courts," in D. Glaser (ed.) Handbook of Criminology. Chicago: Rand McNally.

——— (1966) Conviction: The Determination of Guilt or Innocence Without Trial. Boston: Little, Brown.

OSTROM, E., W. BAUGH, R. GUARASCI, R. B. PARKS, and G. P. WHITAKER (1973) Community Organization and the Provision of Police Services. Beverly Hills, CA: Sage.

PACKER, H. L. (1968) The Limits of the Criminal Sanction. Stanford, CA: Stanford University Press.

REINARMAN, C. and D. MILLER (1975) Direct Financial Assistance to Parolees. Research Report No. 55. Sacramento: California Department of Corrections.

ROSETT, A. and D. R. CRESSEY (1976) Justice by Consent. Philadelphia: Lippincott.

SCHRAG, C. (1977) Review of "Thinking About Crime," "Punishing Criminals," and "We Are the Living Proof." Criminology: 569-573.

STANKO, E. A. (1977) "The arrest versus the case." Paper presented to Society for Study of Social Problems, Chicago.

SUDNOW, D. (1965) "Normal crimes: sociological features of the penal code in a public defender's office." Social Problems 12: 255-276.

U.S. Department of Labor (1977) Unlocking the Second Gate: The Role of Financial Assistance in Reducing Recidivism among Ex-Prisoners. R & D. Monograph 44. Washington, DC: U.S. Department of Labor, Employment and Training Administration.

VAN DEN HAAG, E. (1975) Punishing Criminals. New York: Basic Books.

VON HIRSCH, A. (1976) Doing Justice: The Choice of Punishments. New York: Hill & Wang.

VOTEY, H. L., Jr. and L. PHILLIPS (1976) "Minimizing the social cost of drug abuse: an economic analysis of alternatives for policy." Policy Sciences 7: 315-336.

WILSON, J. Q. (1975) Thinking About Crime. New York: Basic Books.

——— (1968) Varieties of Police Behavior. Cambridge, MA: Harvard University Press.

ZEISEL, H. (1977) "The deterrent effect of the death penalty: facts v. faiths," in P. B. Kurland (ed.) The Supreme Court Review, 1976. Chicago: Univ. of Chicago Press.

8

NOTHING FAILS
LIKE A LITTLE SUCCESS

SIMON DINITZ
Ohio State University

he liberal-reformist impulse in criminology and corrections institutionalized a century ago in the 1870 Declaration of Principles in Cincinnati by what is now the American Correctional Association, and nourished by the New Penology which surfaced under that glorious title around 1935, is now utterly spent. Intellectually, the reformist impulse was made respectable by the victory of positivism over classicism, by empiricism over speculative philosophy, by the clinical over the legal perspective, by causal ambiguity over legal certainty, and by elevating the actor over his act. On the policy level, this liberal-reformist impulse focused, to the exclusion of nearly all else, on humanizing the prisons and jails and on rehabilitating the inmates. To these lofty ends, the new penologists, a mixed bag of crusty prison wardens and other-worldly academic types, supported by a cast of moral entrepreneurs, humanists, clergy, concerned laity, and cause-oriented persons of all descriptions, changed the system in big and little ways—from the creation of the juvenile court system and the implementation of probation and parole, to the elimination of mail censorship and the introduction of small amenities into the drab and unstimulating lives of the incarcerated. A full recital of these changes would be long and impressive. The list, in recent years, includes the revision of state penal codes and the medieval conceptions they harbored, bringing legal and due process

procedures into the prison milieu, using volunteers in probation and throughout the system, former inmates as agents of
reform, the abolition of corporal and, for a few years, capital
punishment, and the development of a great variety of ineffective prevention programs. This truncated list hardly does
justice to the silent and often unpublicized changes wrought in
the last century.

As in any debate or political campaign the incumbent points
with pride, the challenger views with alarm. Despite the im-
provements, any reasonable review might fairly conclude that
the correctional systems, both juvenile and adult, are probably
in poorer shape today than in the heady period of New Penology usually dated 1935-1950. Giving the reformer the edge, they
are only marginally better. One must ask, however, whether
they would be tolerable at all were it not for the New Penology
and the quiet but persistent agitation for reform. That the same
failure to alter the system systematically prevails in nearly
every other aspect of the health, education, and welfare complex is little consolation. Ideas, and the practices which flow
from them, are rooted in the material and organizational
climate of the times. Such is the present climate that reform,
in the traditional sense, has run its course. The question is,
"why?"

First, the liberal-reformist impulse was hacked to death by
its own modest successes no less than by the upheavals of the
civil rights, antiwar, urban, and student revolts which shook
American society to its very foundations in the twenty years
after the Brown v. Board of Education decision of the Supreme
Court in 1954. For the moment, at least, the evolutionary
impulse in criminology, like a spent candle, flickers ever so
tenuously. The liberal impulse, to push the flickering candle
metaphor, is almost but not quite burned out. Neither the
radical rhetoric, devoid of solid scholarship, nor the neoclassical resurgence, an exercise in sterile syllogisms, has or will
destroy it, although both flanks of this movement have already
achieved noteworthy and necessary changes. Critical crimi-

nology has again called attention to the systemic rather than individual nature of our problems; neoclassicism to the need for redress of the social defense-offender treatment balance. The radical view surfaced, quite obviously, in response to the inequities of a social system which produces some winners and all too may losers; neoclassicism resurfaced as a response to this radical challenge and to the increasingly justifiable paranoia about crime in the streets committed by these socially processed losers.

Second, the liberal-reformist impulse was a response to the technological revolution which destroyed the old social order—the "cake of custom" so cherished by Sumner, the *Gemeinschaft* of Tonnies, and the social integration of Durkheim. This reformist impulse flowered as masses of rootless and uprooted people, immigrants and migrants, seeking to reconstruct their lives, descended on our cities and towns. When private philanthropy proved inadequate, to say nothing of being patronizing, the preconditions existed for the institutionalization of this reformist ideal in education, in health, in employment, and in criminal justice.

Third, dissatisfaction with the prevailing social order received yet another jolt—the ascendancy of Freudian, neo-Freudian and pseudo-Freudian doctrines as the explanatory framework for the massive personal disorganization and pathology during much of this century. Overlooking, for the moment at least, the cool reception accorded Freudian dogma for several decades after the introduction of psychoanalysis to a stunned and unbelieving medical profession, this pyschoanalytic perspective, coupled with the decay of traditional social institutions, may be said to constitute the basis of the rehabilitation and reform ethic.

Fourth, the postindustrial society gave rise to our quasi-welfare state—the Swedenization of America—incorporating just about every element of Norman Thomas' Socialist platform planks via the New, Fair, Square, and other Deals and Frontiers except, of course, for public ownership of the means and fruits of production. The social welfare tradition is now deeply embedded in American life. The Fabian views have been translated into conventional policies and practices and, more to the point, into the conventional wisdom of the social and policy scientist. In corrections, I can think of no recommendation in the 1870 Declaration of Principles which is not now in place. Such is the fickle nature of the health, education, and welfare industry in this country (and HEW is one of the largest of our enterprises) that many of the glories attained by the liberal-reformist tradition—indeterminate sentences, educational, psychological, and classification services, various elaborations of psychotherapeutic intervention, the special handling of juveniles—are now under fire; some, like the parole system, are in the process of being dismantled in favor of mandatory sentences. Yesterday's humaneness is today's patronization of the defenseless. The historic fight for the right to treatment has become today's struggle for the right to be left alone. Yesteryear's belief in rehabilitation has been thoroughly undercut by the reintroduction of the three horsemen of penal history—punishment, deterrence, and incapacitation.

In short, the string has run out on the reformist position. Ameliorative efforts have alleviated some of the grosser inequities of the criminal justice system. Piecemeal efforts at reform have been just that—successful in minor ways. Most correctional reformers, like most old New Dealers, are older and possibly wiser. They are also more pessimistic, discouraged, and disenchanted by their failure to create a more just, fair, and humane system. The questions now are not whether we fight the new death penalty laws in the states in which they have been enacted, replace the megaprisons, whether we abolish parole, and how we recruit, train and pay for better staff. These are still open questions, to be sure, but all seem unimportant to that gallant and exhausted band of aging dreamers. The central issue now has little to do with nostrums and panaceas. The current concern is whether the criminal justice system is to function as the ultimate repository for the social misfits and the déclassé whose labor and existence are redundant in our postindustrial world. If it is to be the ultimate warehouse, then no amount of conjugal visiting, work, educational and home furloughs, fixed net sentences, lowered age of adulthood (16, 14) or other reforms in the prison or in the subsystems of law enforcement, prosecution, and courts will promote the return of such superfluous persons to the mainstream of American life. As an academic and a reformer with bona fide credentials for swimming against the current, I think the time has come to give up on our earlier claims and face the ultimate temporal reality: unless drastic alterations occur in postmodern society, the health, welfare, and educational sectors will fail to reform, to educate, and to provide the decent health services which many western European societies seem so much better able to furnish. The dilemma is this: either we lower our expectations and accept social inequality, stratification, and deprivation in our social system, or we recast present society radically and dramatically. The neoclassicists argue the inevitability of the former, the critical criminologists the latter. Neither group knows its history any too well. Both extremes will soon depart the scene, much like other historical oddities. In the meantime, a frustrated and fearful public looks to its experts for guidance— experts too honest, too committed, or too discouraged to offer all but the most prosaic recommendations for reshaping the prison and the system of which it is so much a part. Improving the lot of inmates is no small matter, of course. But the many recommendations for reform are not going to fundamentally alter a system which has a dearth of options.

THE FALL AND RISE OF THEORIES

In the absence of a verified body of knowledge, criminology has consisted of one etiological and correctional bandwagon after another. Most such theories, chiefly the organic, have mercifully departed the scene quietly after a rapid rise and slow burn-out. I refer, by way of illustration, to the Dugdale and Goddard abominations stemming from their respective work on the Jukes and Kallikaks; the rise and fall of the EEG fad which produced so many tracings and so little substance; and, most recently, to the tumult and great expectations arising from the discovery of the XYY chromosome and, in a different context, of methadone treatment. Indeed, this faddism may be traced back to the phrenologists, the constitutional inferiority writers, the earlier "juicers" or hormonal researchers, the Lange, Rosanoff heredity as destiny European school, the Glueck type of eclectics, and the various brands of determinists and free willers.

One principle defies refutation in the history of criminological thought. This principle is that any perspective, no matter how outlandish, tends to surface over and over again in the guise and terminology appropriate to its temporal resurrection. Thus, sociobiology is back in the person of Edward O. Wilson. The earlier "juicers" are back; the Pavlovians now parade under the banner of behavior modifiers, and the bell which produced salivation in the dog is now called the reinforcer. The dysgenic and drift theories have been repackaged by Jensen, Shockley, Herrnstein and their colleagues as well as by highly respected researchers such as Mednick, Kallmann, Christiansen and others. An in-depth review of this cyclicity of ideas dressed in the newest verbal fashions has been explored by Ysabel Rennie (1978) in her book *The Search for Criminal Man*. But Rennie is by no means the first to document the ebb and flow of theories in criminology and, more importantly, their incorporation in penal law and correctional policy.

A second outstanding characteristic of the criminological enterprise is the propensity for modern scholars to forego hard scholarly work in order to assume leadership roles in the intoxicating world of social and ideological movements. Such has too often occurred to the detriment of the scholars and the field. In only a few historical periods was it considered inappropriate for intellectual types to get involved in sociopolitical movements. In these periods scholarly productivity frequently blossomed, in stark contrast to the present when the media consume ideas like prisons consume people.

THE AMERICAN CONTRIBUTION

The Chicago school, the first authentic American view, was a derivation of the Social Gospel movement among white, small town, Protestant reformers responding to the hordes of immigrants and to the accelerating process of urbanization. The Chicagoans wanted to return to the *Gemeinschaft* of the small midwestern or New England communities from which they came. Origins aside, Albion Small, Lester Ward, W. I. Thomas, E. A. Ross, Robert Park, Ernest Burgess, Walter Reckless, E. L. Faris and many others paved the way for the emergence of nearly all non-Marxist sociological perspectives. Drawing on a variety of European social-political theorists— Weber, Durkheim, Spencer, Tarde—the Chicago school evolved a perspective which, above all, focused on a consensus and integration as the "normal" state of social organization and within this cohesive context, a limited amount of deviant behavior as necessary and functional to the social system.

The Chicagoans' emphasis on cohesion found in these unassimilated millions the naive human resources for Zangwill's unfulfilled and probably unfulfillable dream of the "melting pot," for universal public education, for the emergence of the juvenile court. The Chicagoans pushed social welfare beyond Hull House and the Educational Alliance. They rejected the old country rigidities of class and clan. They placed their bets on social mobility and meritocracy as the basis for progress and the amelioration of social problems. Above all, the Chicago view was optimistic. There were ends to be achieved, problems to be solved, progress to be made. Technology, according to Ogburn, was the genie. It would create an un-imagined range of problems (and in this he was surely correct). But this same genie would also provide the solutions. The time discrepancy between the appearance of the technical block-buster and its containment was dubbed "culture lag"—a con-cept which, unfortunately, is now out of vogue.

The Chicago school came to focus on social disorganization as the key element in deviance. By social disorganization Shaw and the rest meant the breakdown of the consensual norms and standards: norms had lost their holding power in the ethnic and national ghettos of the largest American cities. This process of the attenuation of earlier norms proved to be the basis for differential association and differential identification, as Sutherland and Glaser were to argue.

Meanwhile, Sellin was dealing with much the same problem of normative disintegration in his justly famous statement on culture conflict and its significance for crime. This position is nowhere more definitively observed than on the current Israeli scene where clashes of religious, cultural, western-nonwestern, modern-traditional groups are not only replicating but reca-pitulating the American experience of the period 1890-1940. As in the United States, far from assimilating this diversity and creating a new man, these conflicts threaten the internal fabric of Israeli life.

In sum, the American ethos and cultural universals em-phasized optimism, modernism, progress, and consensus. American criminology drank deeply of this intoxicating brew. Conflict only afflicted the old world with its silly national, religious and ethnic antagonisms. There was nothing inherent in society which a lot of good will and a pinch of technical know-how could not set aright.

Similarly, the American ethos rejected the cold-blooded rationality of utilitarianism. Ours was, after all, a compas-sionate society. An examination of the early textbooks in sociology demonstrates convincingly a preoccupation not with class and ideology, but with such social problems as alcoholism, crime, poverty, racial injustice, mental retardation, and prostitution. In short, dependent, disruptive, and deviant people were the problems. Major institutional change was neither necessary nor warranted. This was substantially true in all areas—from the legal and economic to the family and educational institutions. The system was assumed to be fair, but no system is perfect; crime, mental illness, and chronic drunkenness are, after all, perfectly normal no matter what the social organization is like. The prescription: leave the system alone and treat the personal pathologies. Rehabilitate, educate, provide insight. Above all, make it possible for the lowliest and most humble of men and women to climb to the top or, at least, to rise.

In practice, the reformers did improve the facilities and care given the three d's,—the dependent, disruptive, and delinquent, if only very modestly. Dix, Beers, and Deutsch took on the mental hostipals; the Wickersham Commission took on crime; Gompers, Hillman, Mitchell, and Lewis the appalling conditions of labor; the Anti-Saloon League, Demon Rum; the Child Savers, the deplorable treatment of delinquent, neglected and abused children; the police, the courts, and the Federal Bureau of Narcotics, the alleged drug problem. Under the New Deal, alphabet agencies proliferated. The coalition put together by the New Dealers consisted of the underprivileged, populists, academics, ethnics, urban (blue collar) workers, and some farmers. It survived long enough to move the United States into the age of the quasi-welfare state—a direction which no one has been able to reverse. Indeed, the tension between the warfare and welfare state merely slowed the movement toward the latter. One need not be a prophet to predict national employment, income, health, and housing standards to replace the present chaos in these areas. If nothing else, the accelerating fiscal bankruptcy of our major cities and counties may push federalization of services as different as education and criminal justice. Revenue sharing, contrary to its stated goals, may be the forerunner of various federalization policies. The liberal impulse, spent in criminology-corrections, is still very much a factor in the formulation of policies in other social areas.

Certain events become benchmarks in human affairs. Often these events are so "silent" that their significance becomes evident only in historical perspective. Such an event was the closing of the American frontier in or about 1890. If Frederick Jackson Turner is to be believed, this closing profoundly and irreversibly altered the American dream. It dampened the unbridled optimism of the times, circumscribed future growth, changed migration patterns, and eventually forced the sovereign states to become the sovereign nation. Greeley's prescription, "Go west, young man," is now answered by the former governor of Oregon who said, in essence, "Stay home, young man."

With all due respect to Frederick Jackson Turner's thesis, an even more notable landmark in the American experience was the successful structural and, to a lesser degree, interpersonal assimilation of the millions of immigrants who were admitted, if not warmly welcomed, to this country. By the end of World War II, the etiology of deviant, disruptive, and dependent conduct could no longer be attributed to social pathology, social disorganization, and culture conflict—shorthand concepts for the acculturation experience and consequences. A profound shift had again occurred in the lay and professional construction of social reality.

It became evident, though usually unsaid, that many of the unassimilated had become the unassimilable. No amount of social intervention could or would melt the "unmeltable" millions in our midst. Behaviorally, and in contradiction to our long professed and much admired ethos, a two-tiered social system took shape. Warner and then Hollingshead began to look at the constituent elements of social class; Hunter initiated the search for community elites; Mills for the power elite. The dam had burst, the unthinkable became speakable.

The realization of the existence and persistence of a semi-permanent underclass of losers with its own ethic, values, goals, and expectations startled the social science community and fragmented it politically. Old "brain trusters" like Moley, Lawrence, and Sokolsky spread the word in their syndicated columns. Respected political sociologists like Lipset, Nisbet, and the *Commentary* circle of Kristol, Podhoretz ("Your Problem and Mine"), Nathan Glaser, Moynihan, and peripheral figures like Himmelfarb agitated the intellectual community. The most recent flap was the turnabout of James Coleman on the effects of busing.

A historian might date the origin of the unmeltable assumption to a most influential book—Whyte's *Street Corner Society*. In discussing the divergent paths taken by the street corner and college groups, Whyte became the forerunner of some of the subcultural and limited opportunity themes later pursued by Cohen, Cloward and Ohlin, Wolfgang and Ferracuti, and Liebow. As Walter Miller elaborated, the underclass has internalized a coherent set of values—trouble, toughness, smartness, expressive goals—conducive to deviant conduct. For Miller it is not position discontent or limited opportunity, though both are real, but rather the lifestyle of segments of the underclass which makes street crimes a virtual underclass monopoly.

This more or less permanent underclass, by implication, and by whatever empirical research has been mustered, is different from the previous sets of underclass groups in two respects: first, it is different qualitatively, and second, the social system seems indisposed to develop new methods to permit the upward circulation of this underclass. On the first count, the new underclass consists of the socioeconomic failures, some four generations deep now, of previous rural migrations to the city. Included, too, are the remnants of earlier immigrant groups. To these must be added the personally disorganized—alcoholics, drug addicts, and the ambulatory mentally ill. The socially created and processed unmeltables consist of the ghetto blacks and Hispanics and, in some parts of the country, the native Americans. This more or less permanent underclass has no voice and no effective vote. This makes them prime targets for political exploitation. More and more isolated in central cities, cut off from community life by inner belts and by the provincialism inherent in their status, the line between class and caste is fading. Few of the poverty and welfare programs have actually touched this sizable underclass. Nothing on the horizon is likely to be more effective.

On the second count, reformers premised their activities on some variation of the Protestant ethic. They assumed an inherent and universal desire for self-improvement. The will was there, the tools lacking. Provide the tools and upward social mobility must and will follow. Current disillusionment with reform, I contend, is related to the shift in the nature of the values ascribed to the underclass. If one rejects upward social mobility as an unattainable goal and is preoccupied with "getting by," the prescriptions of the reformers seem odd, indeed. Education and vocational training offer little to people who have already failed repeatedly in our schools. One can afford the luxury of the latest therapeutic games, like primal screams, when other needs have been met. Even behavior modification, through either positive reinforcement or aversive conditioning, works more poorly with the underclass group. In short, our individually oriented rehabilitation programs do not and cannot reach the caste-like underclass.

Even more depressing to reformers has been the collapse of consensus on what constitutes a desirable and normative lifestyle. Sinful and immoral conduct gave way to abnormal, pathological, aberrant, criminal, and disorganized behavior in the 1930s which became deviant in the 1950s and merely variant in the late 1960s and 1970s. Our tolerance has markedly increased for variant lifestyles, however outlandish. We accept as normal that which we only recently abhorred as sinful. We are fearful of being perceived as square and straight—the new outsiders of our time. We can now conclude with Erasmus that when everything is possible, nothing is true. If so, what and who stands in need of rehabilitation? Lynd once asked, in a most provocative volume, "education for whom?" The penal reformers face the same problem: "rehabilitation for what?" Many have unfortunately concluded that little or no special education is required to remain a loser, a never-will-be, a permanent outsider with a variant lifestyle. I submit that, more than any other development, the American acceptance and even celebration of deviance has mortally undercut the zeal of our reformers. How can they expect conformity to ambiguous norms when their own children are frequently part of the increasingly variant family arrangements and unusual sex patterns which are so contrary to our moral legacy? Presently only zealots can be certain of the rectitude of their ways. In a world of competing norms and life patterns, who has the temerity to proclaim the truth—to define, let alone implement, the people-changing ideal?

The failure of rehabilitation has been trumpeted by Lipton, Martinson, and Wilks. Martinson's comment that "nothing works" is a succinct if unpleasant and overstated conclusion. Parallel pessimism applies to compensatory and related education programs and to conventional programs dealing with alcoholics and addicts. Other examples abound in all areas of counseling and therapy. The solution, however, is not in polemical Marxist prescriptions or a return to eighteenth-century verities.

For the reform impulse to make a difference once again will require fundamental attention to the needs of the lower class unmeltables. Those of us who have melted successfully are incapable of understanding the focal concerns of those who have not and cannot do likewise. The programs must be elaborated by the losers. The classic reformer—prosperous, educated, informed, well-meaning—is an anachronism. The world has passed him by. He himself is likely to be anything but a straight. At the very least he is probably unconventional and is as troubled by his "problems of living" as those he seeks to reform.

In summary, I have argued three points:

1. The liberal-reformist movement in corrections has succeded in implementing most of its ideas and programs. The impulse is spent and most of the reformers are sadly disillusioned that their schemes have created no utopia.

2. The characteristics of the at-risk populations, especially the underclass, are markedly different now than in the past when the Protestant ethic and the inevitability of progress were perceived as being American monopolies. Indeed, the cores of the largest and even some of the middle-sized cities are becoming huge reservations for blacks and other déclassé groups, including the aged and handicapped. If it is true, and I believe Miller is generally correct in his assessment of the differential values of the social classes, then the nature of our problem is qualitatively different than that in the past. We have a new and largely transplanted underclass of unmeltables. We also have an overabundance of self-proclaimed outsiders who refuse to accept many of the conventional standards as personally binding.

3. The approaches with which we felt comfortable in the past—self-improvement, social reintegration, psychological intervention—are consequently futile avenues for major reform. Unless and until we develop new conceptions, penal reformers are likely to continue to support recommendations for change which are superficial and largely cosmetic.

REFERENCE

RENNIE, Y. (1978) The Search for Criminal Man. Boston: Heath.

9

CRIMINOLOGY AND CRIMINAL JUSTICE IN AMERICA
Fact or Fantasy

CHARLES L. NEWMAN
University of Texas at Arlington

ecently I came across an old clipping from the *Wall Street Journal* (regrettably the date of publication was not noted) which illustrates the problem of the criminal justice system. The unidentified author writes:

> A reporter for a North Carolina newspaper was summoned to district court in Winston-Salem recently and when he arrived the judge announced, "I have a present for you." Whereupon he summoned five men who had been convicted of public drunkenness and released them in the reporter's custody.

> It seems he was reacting to an earlier story the reporter had written calling attention to the judge's unusual sentence ordering seven drunks, including several of the five in question, dropped off at the county line. Instead of vamoosing out of town, they hitched a ride back to Winston-Salem. That's when the jurist decided to turn them over to the reporter. "It's entirely different when one theorizes these problems and when one sits on the bench and has to do something about them," he said.

> The judge obviously has a point. As the late Sam Rayburn once put it, "Any jackass can kick down a barn, but it takes a good carpenter to build one."

For the past several decades, the problems of criminal justice have maintained a significant portion of our nation's attention. Crime has always fascinated us. Our daily television diet of crime programming, whether in fantasy or the local and national news, supports this notion. It is unlikely that we could discover any era in human history in which so much human energy and attention by the public media has been devoted to the problems of law and order.

Yet, in spite of the billions of spoken and printed words, the work of several presidential commissions, the activity of federal, state, and local criminal justice agencies and planning commissions, the multimillion-dollar investments of LEAA, the thousands of criminological research pieces and expositions replete with rhetoric, we have not produced an empirically validated statement on the cause of crime, nor has a national strategy to deal with offenders been developed. Without an understanding of cause, it is unlikely that a "cure" will be forthcoming.

This is not to suggest that efforts have not been made, for various experimental programs in enforcement and corrections have indeed demonstrated that we can have an impact upon some law violators under certain circumstances, given the appropriate set of offenders and appropriate supply of resources, i.e., personnel, facilities, and programs.

Many in criminology accept the proposition that crime is deeply embedded in the social structure of our society and that only with the eradication of poverty, unemployment, and discrimination—problems which are presumed to constitute the major breeding ground of conventional crime—can we even begin to hope for any turn-around in the escalating crime problem.

The reality is that there are substantial numbers of people who, while involuntary participants in our systems, appear to have neither the desire nor the capacity to lead law-abiding lives. Some of these people enjoy the protected environment which keeps them from maintaining themselves in the free world on a day-to-day basis. Anyone who is familiar with local jails knows the character who uses the jail as his "home away from home." No matter how inadequate the jail may be, whether in facilities, program, or staff, the certainty of bed and board for this type of individual is far more important than any restrictions that the system imposes on him. Do not misunderstand my point. I am not suggesting that we retain archaic, inadequate facilities because they represent for some prisoners a place better than home. What I am saying is that we cannot hold corrections responsible for the failures of such individuals, though we can provide jails and prisons which are fit for human habitation and provide basic civil rights for those incarcerated.

Then there are a substantial number of individuals who see the risk of incarceration as the social price of their illicit activities. Such individuals, contrary to the misguided belief, are neither sick nor capable of being resocialized. They will do their time, and they will be back again, if caught. Crime, for them, is profitable.

Even more critical to the criminal justice field is the growing public expectation that the police and corrections must bear the burden of dealing with an increasing number of individuals who represent a new pattern of dissidence. Many of these dissidents are the people who warmed to the expectation that a better world and a better life for themselves was emerging, only to discover that the political rhetoric of the New Deal, the Great Society, the Fair Deal, and other promises of hope did not include delivery, or at least in sufficient magnitude to represent any major change in the free community. But institutions, with court insistence, are now being pressured to provide services, such as health care, which the free community has been unwilling to make available to all of its citizens.

In addition to the past failure to deliver promised resources, there is the tragedy of our national scandals which have evoked both a distrust of elected officials and a questioning of constituted authority to serve the public good. Police officers find evidence of this on the street, college professors experience it in the classroom, and certainly correctional administrators and personnel have not been immune from the problem.

THE SEARCH FOR INSTANT SOLUTIONS

We have no great difficulty in identifying the problems confronting criminal justice. The difficulty seems to be in finding solutions which do not create greater problems in themselves. For example, in the effort to reduce crime in the streets, preventive detention has been offered as a solution. But the "medicine" proves worse than the "illness," when we consider the long-range potential damage to all of our personal liberties.

In our search for instant answers to complex problems, the solutions have often been oversold, with the consequent disillusionment over the value of new strategies. This is especially true in the areas which have attempted to redefine the offender as a sick person, with all of the consequences of psychiatric manipulations. Not infrequently, treatment programs have been offered without theoretical rationale or solid empirical support. The law violator is at once a biosocial being living in a society of laws, values, and responsibilities. Yet, intervention strategies do not relate to the total person, but rather view the offender from the perspective of economic or political influences, genetic misconstruction, opportunity blockage, superego malformation, peer malinfluence, or discrimination. Regrettably, American criminology has done little to shed much light on the problem, and indeed may have impeded progress by failing to interact with criminal justice.

Curiously, when imprisonment was first introduced in this country at the insistence of social reformers, it was represented as a more helpful and productive method of dealing with offenders than death or exile for serious crimes, whipping or mutilation for lesser offenses.

About the same time that prisons were offered as a humane approach to dealing with offenders, other forms of congregate living had been developed to deal with other problem areas. Almshouses served the aged; workhouses, the unemployed; orphanages provided homes for destitute children; insane asylums were established for the mentally aberrant. Congregate institutionalization, whatever the problem, was seen as the most productive approach.

We lived within that frame of reference for well over a century, but gradually a new philosophy began to emerge. The almshouses were replaced by family assistance. Unemployment compensation now substitutes for workhouses. Public and private orphanages have been replaced by Aid to Dependent Children grants and foster homes. Slowly, institutions housing the mentally ill have given way to community-based mental health settings.

In short, our heavy reliance upon isolation of some problem people from the community is becoming increasing less in vogue, and less the desired mode for the delivery of human services. The reasons are, of course, obvious: congregate institutions have proved to be expensive to operate, unable to attain objectives except for confinement, and in many instances counterproductive to the solution of human problems. But the use of secure custody for some individuals is appropriate; the task is to pick the right people to confine and the right mode of confinement. American criminology has done little to provide sound information upon which to base such decisions.

As a consequence, this nation's reliance in dealing with the public offender is still heavily weighted on the side of jails and prisons. Since we do not know who should be confined, we have tried to disguise the prison image behind such nice sounding terms as "detention center," "development facility," or "community correctional center." Sadly, one of the most violent of prison massacres took place not too long ago in a California facility for dangerous offenders euphemistically called an "adjustment center." More important, we have no agreed upon criteria for determining the relative success of the "cure."

Changing the name over the door of a reformatory, calling it a "children's care facility," does not alter the way it functions, unless we are willing to change both the way the service is delivered to the recipient and the way that the recipient is viewed as a human being.

Admittedly, changes have been made in corrections over the past several decades. But by and large, the depersonalization of people in prisons remains unchanged. Even in newer institutions the emphasis seems to be on warehousing, restriction of movement, and generally enforced idleness. Probation and parole continue to be ritualistic procedures, with the primary emphasis still on reporting.

All of this leads me to a consideration of the question of what corrections is all about, where should we be going, and how can we attain those goals.

WHAT, THEN, IS CORRECTIONS?

At first glance, the question appears to be naive. Corrections is that part of the criminal justice system which deals with the offender subsequent to conviction but prior to release to the community. In many states, the nomenclature refers specifically to the institutional component. Elsewhere, it includes probation and parole. But whatever its administrative organization, we recognize that corrections comes at the end of the criminal justice cycle and is often left with the task of tryng to resolve dilemmas passed on to it by law enforcement agents and the courts.

A logical conclusion to be drawn at this point, then, is that the success of corrections as an enterprise is in large measure conditioned by the efficient and effective operation of preceding steps in the justice operation.

CORRECTIONS, THE POLICE, AND THE COURTS

Our success in detection and apprehension has left much to be desired. Not only have we been unsuccessful in making arrests for crimes we know about, there is considerable evidence to support the contention that the level of criminal activity is significantly greater than the number which comes to official attention. But corrections deals only with those who are convicted, and no one can deny the reality of a prisoner's feeling of frustration that *he* got the "short end of the stick" with a commitment, when he knows that other offenders were neither identified by the police nor convicted by the court for similar or other offenses equal to, or worse than, his own.

Moreover, in the majority of jurisdictions, according to the National Advisory Commission on Criminal Justice Standards and Goals, the sentencing decision as to where and how an offender may spend the next years of his or her life is made by a judge whose discretion is not checked, guided by validated criteria, or subject to appellate review. The laws governing the selection of appropriate sentencing alternatives are chaotic. In some states, the court is allowed no discretion regarding mandatory sentencing. In other states, the judge has options as to the nature and extent of the sentence to impose. Whether the judge makes the appropriate choice is based on the willingness to obtain as much information as possible from as many valid sources as possible to match the offender and the sentence. The willingness and capacity to make appropriate choices, however, is quite different from the *right* to make choices in the first place. But whether the judge's choice is restricted or optional, based on personal bias or well-designed information, the fact is that, whatever the decision, it will have a significant impact upon both the offender and the correctional system.

It is also a fact that criminologists have been all too slow in pointing out to the community that the sentencing process impacts upon the success or failure of corrections. We have been even more hesitant to demand a level of competency for judges who mete out penalties. We have ignored almost totally our obligation to point up the fact that the legislative branch bears a large responsibility for the incoherent sentencing policy in most jurisdictions. The fact is that statutes provide little guidance to protect against disparity in sentencing or procedures to prevent abuse or capricious action.

THE CHALLENGES THAT FACE US

The first challenge to criminology and criminal justice is to develop a unified field concept which both describes the problems facing us in a similar manner and seeks solutions to achieve similar goals. Both must be equally concerned that the quality of law enforcement is such that it produces certainty of arrest when an illegal act is committed and a guarantee of conviction in a fair and speedy trial, if guilty. Tragically, neither of these conditions prevails today.

The second challenge relates to the need to develop a common philosophy to be shared by all who work in criminology and criminal justice. As things stand, police officials tend to feel threatened by any viewpoint which presents the offender as anything other than an enemy of society; lawyers and judges act in terms of classical interpretation of crime, in which the law violator is seen as a free moral agent who must pay a suitable penalty for his crime. Social workers, psychologists, psychiatrists, and other mental health workers are inclined to blame society rather than the individual for his offenses, or at least feel that their task of dealing with human beings should not be affected or impeded by any of the constraints of the system in which they work. Custodial personnel are content to respond to the public demand that the offender be held, with custody as the end in itself.

For the most part, criminology has remained aloof from the problems of criminal justice. What it has produced is a plethora of scholarly works which decry the state of the social environment, or describe, in global or minute terms, the historical, genetic, biosocial, or environmental condition of the offender. In some instances, these descriptions, with their refined statistical manipulations, do provide an accurate portrayal of the individuals or events under consideration. More often than not, however, such studies neither advance our understanding of causation nor provide any guidelines for action which can be utilized in dealing with offender groups.

There are those who would contend that the accumulation of criminological knowledge is a legitimate end in itself. Perhaps so, in an era which could afford the luxury of monastic inquiry. That kind of world no longer exists, and partnership between criminological researchers and criminal justice practitioners must be attained.

There are some who will say that such a partnership is beyond achievement. Sooner or later, we are going to have to decide what it is that criminology and criminal justice are to accomplish; what are their social ends and purposes; which of the professional disciplines is to carry leadership responsibility; which of the professional areas will provide the adjunct services. This means, first, that all persons who function within the criminal justice cycle must see a common purpose in their work. That common purpose is the restoration of the offender to the community with a somewhat more acceptable pattern of behavior than was indicated by the delinquent act. Second, this unification suggests a more common bond with the traditions of a larger society which bases its values upon the ultimate worth of the individual in society, regardless of the specific act which may have set the individual apart.

The lack of an integrated philosophy in criminology and criminal justice, the struggle to establish a dominant position as to method, and the competition between phases of the criminal justice cycle are not accidental occurrences, nor should they be naively interpreted as merely someone's inability to "see things right." Nor is this a situation which can be resolved by simple discussion and persuasion. Part of our problem stems from the burden of history. But the largest share of the contemporary difficulty stems from a vacuum in leadership.

CONCLUSION

We are long past the time when we can continue the isolation of the criminal justice field from academic criminology. We must work together, and the mechanism which can forge such a partnership is a faculty of criminology which is broad-based in terms of function, interdisciplinary in terms of theoretic reference, and involved with the criminal justice system as researchers, teachers, planners, and consultants. Similarly, persons from the field can bring to the classroom a vast array of information regarding the realities of criminal justice practice. The extent of mutual cooperation is limited only by our breadth of vision.

10

DEVELOPING A NATIONAL CRIME POLICY
The Impact of Politics on Crime in America

WALTER C. RECKLESS
Ohio State University

HARRY E. ALLEN
San Jose State University

While few Americans in general and criminal justice personnel in particular may perceive it, since 1965 the United States has been formulating a rapidly crystallizing national crime policy which has both broad and far-reaching ramifications for public policy and American society. This national crime policy is a dominant mechanism for asserting federal influence in this problem area, and the political right has a monopoly over the crime issue. We are concerned here with briefly describing the process by which the national crime policy has been articulated, what it is, its impact on research, and what the future might probably be in the last two decades of the twentieth century.

UNKIND AND UNUSUAL POLITICS

In the 1964 presidential campaign, Caplan (1973) has suggested that challenger Barry Goldwater was advised by

AUTHORS' NOTE: *An earlier draft of this paper was presented by one of the authors at the 1978 National Conference of Lambda Alpha Epsilon: American Criminal Justice Association, Dayton, Ohio.*

one-time Attorney General Richard D. Kleindienst to make law and order his principal issue in the campaign against the incumbent, President Lyndon Johnson. Crime was at that time a nonissue. It may have been argued that it was possible, given careful manipulation, to develop a power base which would catapult Goldwater to the presidency by focusing on public concerns in the light of such emerging forces and factors as racism, the nascent but developing urban reservations for the economically disadvantaged, the civil rights movement, ghettoization of urban cores and accompanying white flight, the difficulties associated with the demographic bulge of 16- to 29-year-olds, the backlash potential, among others.

Goldwater did in fact make the crime problem his major issue in a politically exploitative campaign in which one could hear such subthemes as violence in the streets, moral decay, law and order, reaction against youth, heightened racism, alienation, anti-civil rights militancy, and an attempt to hold Johnson personally responsible for such undesirable factors. Goldwater promised—although not too specifically—to do something about the "social issue" he was describing. Such general themes, Walker (1978) and Finckenauer (1978) noted, were later to be repeated in varying but pronounced degrees by George Wallace, Richard Nixon, Gerald Ford, and Ronald Reagan. Even Hubert Humphrey and Henry Jackson eventually accepted the conservative, law-and-order approach and, in a spectacular fence-sitting venture, Carter embraced both the conservative and liberal positions, although on separate issues.

It could be argued that it has been the fear of crime—and the increased number of crimes of violence coupled with urban riots, anti-war radicalism, and prison riots and disturbances (such as Attica)—which has fed the "crisis syndrome" in America and in large part led to the development of the national crime policy. What may happen if the rate of violent crime continues to decrease, as indicated in Table 1, is still undetermined.

TABLE 1
Crime Index Trends in the United States
1973-1978[a]

Year	Types of Crime		
	Violent	Property	Total
1974/1973	+4	+16	+15
1975/1974	+18	+18	+18
1976/1975	−6	+4	+3
1977/1976	−3	−9	−9
1978/1977	−1	−5	−4

a. SOURCE: Federal Bureau of Investigation, **Uniform Crime Reports: January-March 1978,** United States Department of Justice, June 29, 1978.

It fell to President Johnson, the consummate politician and the New Deal cum Great Society advocate, to legitimate crime as a social issue, which he effected in a politically expedient move and as a liberal. Determined to preempt the conservatives, Johnson seized the initiative by making Goldwater's concern about crime his own and appointed a presidential commission to study the problems of crime, instructing the commission to speak to "correct" issues. He really did not want to involve the federal government here. War on crime did not fit in at all well with his Great Society, would run counter to the long American tradition of treating crime as a local problem and thus a local responsibility, and could inflame the public if they perceived it as a movement to develop a national police force, anathema in American politics. He would have by far favored an answer to the crime problem which was predicated on the anti-poverty and education components, on equal opportunity and equal rights, on the reduction of unemployment, and similar measures. Johnson yielded to political expediency and thus legitimized crime as a national political issue.

Johnson was also undoubtedly aware that the federal government could do some things: form a commission, study the problem, propose reforms, provide later financial and technical assistance, and provide leadership through tightening and increasing the effectiveness of the federal criminal justice system, including the passage of new laws and the overhauling of the federal criminal code.

The President's Commission on Law Enforcement and Administration of Justice delivered a set of documents containing over 400 recommendations, not put forth in the form of priorities, but incorporating the Great Society perspective and focusing on institutional change and system reform. These 1967 documents—coming in a year when only $30 million of federal funds were being devoted to criminal justice research, evaluation, demonstration and innovation—quickly catapulted larger appropriations for the Law Enforcement Assistance Administration, reaching $641 million in the 1978-1979 fiscal year.

The important issue is not that one politician attacked and the other countered, but that certain conservatives have, for political, exploitative, and self-aggrandizing purposes, persistently articulated a proposed crime policy which has been accepted as the national policy; that liberals have (for much the same reasons) accepted that policy; and that future trends are now rather predictable, for the articulated national policy prevents a radical rethinking of the problem. What is the conservative policy? How does it differ from the liberal position? And why has the conservative policy gained ascendancy?

LIBERAL VERSUS CONSERVATIVE POLITICAL PHILOSOPHY

Insofar as criminal justice is involved, liberals can be distinguished from conservatives in the extent of their estimate of the ability of the criminal justice system to control and deter crime. Liberals, in general, believe that human behavior is determined by the socioeconomic environment and that, as such, crime can best be addressed through federal action programs which reflect high priority social objectives achieved through social engineering and such social reforms as the civil rights acts, Equal Rights Amendment, youth conservation corps, programs to train unemployed youth, anti-poverty activities, and delinquency prevention efforts and experiments.

Liberals are thus less optimistic about the potential of the justice system and thus less likely to emphasize deterrent and preventive components in the administration of criminal justice. They are more concerned with and traditionally emphasize the amount of fairness in the criminal justice process, in programs to help and rehabilitate the offender and to prevent delinquency, and in social programs and projects which would attack the "root causes" of crime. Packer (1968) has suggested other specific areas of difference when he speaks about the crime control and the due process models of the American criminal justice system.

Students of the criminal justice system could quickly identify certain other components which would characterize the liberal position. In brief, these would be:

(1) Crime arises from social circumstances which governments can ameliorate.
(2) Offenders commit crime due to such social factors as poverty, lack of education, or racism, for example.
(3) One should engage in war on poverty, not on crime which is a symptom of the problem.
(4) It is essential to eliminate slums and ghettoes and to improve the inner cities.
(5) Governments should provide jobs and opportunities.
(6) The stress should be on crime and justice, not on law and order.
(7) One should provide equitable treatment throughout the social order.
(8) Crime cannot be controlled by increasing the effectiveness and efficiency of the criminal justice system.

(9) It is desirable to advocate and implement such tactics and programs as gun control, decriminalization of victimless crimes, community-based corrections, work and education release and furlough, and parole contracts.

(10) One should pursue distributive justice.

Conservatives, as a group, tend to be much more optimistic about the potential capacity of the system and see promise for reversing crime trends through such approaches as "swift and certain trials," less regard for rules of procedure, and mandatory and stiffer sentences.

The conservative position tends to reflect what in 1968 Nixon called retributive justice: since criminal behavior is rooted in the defects of human beings and persons are responsible for their own acts, offenders ought to receive their just deserts. This position would include, *inter alia*:

1. It is the nature of humankind to exercise free will, and thus offenders must get their just deserts.
2. We must have law and order, but not crime.
3. The liberal Supreme Court decisions have handcuffed law enforcement, pampered offenders, and caused us to lose sight of victims.
4. Offenders should face the presumption of guilt.
5. Punishment deters others as well as the instant offender.
6. One should advocate and implement such tactics as
   A. conspiracy statutes
   B. electronic surveillance and wire tapping
   C. preventive detention
   D. capital punishment
   E. authorization of "no knock" searches
   F. opposition to gun control
   G. increased numbers of law enforcement officers
   H. elimination of bail for heroin traffickers and hard narcotics sellers
   I. abolition of parole and restriction of community-based corrections

J. mandatory sentences, including
- (1) mandatory *minimum* sentences for
  - (a) use of a gun in a crime
  - (b) repeat offenders who commit crimes of violence
  - (c) sale of heroin
- (2) mandatory *death* sentences for
  - (a) political terrorists
  - (b) war-related treason
  - (c) sabotage
  - (d) airplane hijacking resulting in death
  - (e) bombing of public buildings
  - (f) killing of a law enforcement officer in the line of duty or of a prison guard by an inmate
  - (g) murder by a hired killer.

See, for example, the discussion by Alper and Weiss (1977) on retribution and the mandatory sentence.

NATIONAL CRIME POLICY AND CRIMINAL JUSTICE RESEARCH

Turning now to the interface between the national crime policy and criminal justice research, it is necessary to note that the primary (but not only) major federal agency supporting research in the criminal justice system is the U.S. Department of Justice. Within the Department of Justice, the major research unit is the National Institute of Law Enforcement and Criminal Justice. Our contention is that the research agenda of the American criminal justice system is substantially defined by this federal agency and the conservative position is strongly reflected therein.

With assistance from its Advisory Committee, the National Institute of Law Enforcement and Criminal Justice conducted a survey of agency heads, practitioners, elected officials, criminal justice researchers, state planners, city/county planners and coordinators, public interest groups, professional associations, and the staff of the Department of Justice and Law Enforcement Assistance Administration. A total of 700 survey forms—listing and describing 10 priority areas to be addressed in their research over a three- to five-year period as defined by the National Institute of Law Enforcement and Criminal Justice—were mailed to the above recipients and a response rate of 47% (330 returned questionnaires) was achieved. What is important here is the ranking of the priority areas: (1) career criminals, (2) deterrence, (3) pretrial processing, and (4) sentencing. Other areas included community crime prevention, violent crime, correlates and determinants of crime, performance standards, rehabilitation, and utilization of police resources, in that order (see Ewing, 1978, for detailed discussion).

What were not listed were research topics identified by Glaser, who addressed the process of defining research agendas and noted:

> In their procedures the initiative in developing proposals is with outside grant applicants, although officials of these government agencies do convey to the scientific community the kinds of research they would like to encourage. This communication is achieved through public speeches at professional meetings, through responses to informal inquiries by prospective grant applicants, and perhaps most effectively, by the types of research that are funded or rejected [1977: 10].

Glaser proposed five potential topics for research to be sponsored by federal agencies:

(1) Experiments in reducing age segregation, such as fostering collaboration between senior citizens, parents, and youth in school, after class hours, or on certain days; sponsoring recreational and hobby activities which integrate a greater age spectrum; and subsidizing employment of youth with adults.
(2) Expanding legitimate achievement opportunities for those maladjusted in school.

(3) Exploring alternative drug policies for heroin, marijuana, tranquilizers, and other psychoactive substances.
(4) Measuring the consequences of reallocating discretion in penalties.
(5) Assessing the impacts of correctional services, focusing on recidivism and correctional programs.

It is apparent that Glaser is in the liberal orientation. The extent to which such liberal thinking will be successful in influencing the National Institute of Law Enforcement and Criminal Justice to implement many of these other research areas and topics remains questionable. We also note an absence of proposed funding for extensive work on white collar crime, organized crime, political corruption, and police corruption.

CONCLUSIONS

We have argued that there is now a national crime policy which reflects the conservative philosophy and that the research agenda in the criminal justice system areas predominantly reflects and is directly defined by that influence. The addition of Nixon's strict constructionists to the U.S. Supreme Court may have created a long-term legacy of the law-and-order strategy.

We could also predict that the federal government will, at least in the next two decades, remain firmly rooted in the criminal justice system research. One notes that the "iron law of political dispersion"[1] has been triggered and the lobbying groups—ranging from law enforcement agencies eager to continue "pork barrel" funding at local levels up to educational units desirous of continuing law enforcement education program funding—have a vested interest in maintaining such federal influence.

Finally, we conclude that the public crime policies of the conservatives are likely to continue well into the future and that one can expect these policies to become embodied in such programs and actions as expediting capital punishment, the abolition of parole, fixed sentencing, and restrictions of community-based corrections. If terrorism spreads to the United States, a not unlikely event, these policies are even more likely to assume more immediate implementation, greatly enhancing the power of the state and decreasing those individual freedoms provided for in the Constitution.

NOTE

1. Iron law of political dispersion refers to the rapid distribution of funds to a large number of recipients, predicated on marshalling sufficient political support for the sponsor to withstand concerted efforts to abolish the program.

REFERENCES

ALPER, B. S. and J. W. WEISS (1977) "The mandatory sentence: recipe for retribution." Federal Probation 41 (December): 15-20.

CAPLAN, G. (1973) "Reflections on the nationalization of crime: 1964-68." Law and the Social Order 3: 583-635.

EWING, B. G. (1978) "Analysis of the 1977 National Institute of Law Enforcement and Criminal Justice Planning Survey." (mimeo)

FINCKENAUER, J. O. (1978) "Crime as a national political issue: 1964-76." Crime and Delinquency 24: 13-27.

GLASER, D. (1977) "The federal government and criminal justice research." Federal Probation 41 (December): 9-14.

PACKER, H. L. (1968) The Limits of the Criminal Sanction. Stanford, CA: Stanford Univ. Press.

WALKER, S. (1978) "Reexamining the President's crime commission: the challenge of crime in a free society after ten years." Crime and Delinquency 24: 1-12.

11

CRIMINOLOGY AND THE
REAFFIRMATION OF HUMANIST IDEALS

EDWARD SAGARIN
City College of New York

ANDREW KARMEN
John Jay College of Criminal Justice

In commenting on the title that so aptly described the work of Alvin Gouldner (1970), Robert Merton (1976) asked when there had not been a crisis, or a coming crisis, in sociology. In fact, is it not true that in the sciences, and specifically the social sciences, crises are not only chronic, but necessary? If on the one hand they are symptomatic of failures to face issues, to make advances, to adjust to new situations, on the other they are manifestations of the recognition of such failures, and they imbue the scientists with a sense of restlessness, of what might be called, to make a rare negative out of a common affirmative, a sense of self-dissatisfaction. It is in such an ambience that creativity, if it is not born, can at least thrive.

Yet, this having been said, it would be delusion to believe that all crises, whether in the sciences or elsewhere, are equally serious, have equal potential for generating disaster. So that if it is true, as can easily be demonstrated, that criminology has been beset not so much by its recurrent coming crises as by its continuity of current ones, this should not be reason to relax with the comforting (or discomforting) thought that things have always been as bad as they are now.

The concerns of criminology have primarily been divisible into two types. One is rooted in the discipline, the fashions and fads that it has entertained, the theories once embraced only to be later abandoned, and the frustration—probably endemic in the social and behavioral sciences—of specialists who cannot agree on a set of principles, rules, explanations, theoretical orientations. It is often repeated that there is healthiness in this sharp conflict of ideas in the scholarly world, but only if the debates are less than endless, if there is some agreement on a level of discourse so that one can proceed to new debate on a higher level, and if the discipline is not as far away from the answers toward which science reaches as it had been decades before. The second type of concern of criminology is rooted in the objective world, specifically the world of crime, and how criminologists perceive it. The era of Prohibition was evidently a time if not of greater crime than before, then at least of crime more sensational, more renowned. The period that started somewhere in the early or mid-years of the 1960s and has continued until this writing (1978) appears to public, to media, to political and cultural leaders, and to at least some criminologists to be marked by extraordinarily high crime rates, by precipitate rises in rates from year to year, at least of official figures, albeit with some occasional fluctuations, a flattening out of a curve for a brief time, even a momentary decline.

These two concerns are of course interrelated. To the extent that criminologists discount the upsurge of crime as a creation of media and politicans, a delusion of the public, there will be a lesser concern with the putative theoretical deficiencies of the discipline. If crime waves are nothing but myths, and organized crime exists only in the minds of journalists seeking front page bylines and law enforcement officers requiring better data for higher budgets, there is more need to reassure and reeducate the public than to find elusive answers to difficult problems. If the surrounding violence is no more than a continuation of the heritage of a nation that was founded on violence against the Indians and later against the British, that marched steadily westward by means of frontier violence, and that reestablished a system of oppression against the former slaves by hooded night riders using rope, tar, and faggot, then there is no new crisis, but only a chronic old one. If the high crime rates for the index offenses are artifacts of improved reporting, better and more sophisticated statistical refinements, and a lesser reluctance on the part of victims to involve themselves in making complaints to the police, then there is no need to increase the worries that were already burdening us.

Nevertheless, save for a minority of criminologists, few people any longer doubt the reality of the present upsurge in crime. Upperworld crime may not have increased, but may only recently have been forced out of its very protective closet, thanks at least in part to the pioneering work of Edwin Sutherland; and there is no reliable way of knowing whether such political crime as bribery has increased and has traveled upward into more and more sacrosanct sectors of American political life, for except for the work of some muckrakers, we have had to rely on information based upon the handful of cases that came to the offices of prosecutors. But streets once safe no longer are; neighborhoods that had not known a single street robbery over a period of years now have them as daily or at least weekly occurrences, and in daylight as well as at night; and despite precautions that have increased exponentially and prudence that sometimes appears to border on rationally induced paranoia, danger from crime is all around us. For those of us who live by an abiding faith in the potential of humanity to survive, endure, and prevail (to use the words chosen by William Faulkner in his famed Nobel acceptance speech), the denial of crime on a large and growing scale, as a dangerous social reality, and the claim that "make our streets safe" is nothing more than a code term for oppression of the lower social classes and the establishment of a police state, is a capitulation to the hardliners, conservatives, and antihumanists. It is to tell those who proclaim that "nothing works" (including, of course, their own funded research, let us not forget) and that we should "lock them up and throw away the keys" that the problem is theirs to solve, much as we may bemoan their solutions.

Sometimes the ideology of liberals and humanists (or radicals, conflict sociologists, and numerous others whom we might mention, and with many of whose aims and views we are deeply sympathetic) appears to be just that: ideology and not science. Here, white collar crime serves as a useful example. It is often said that white collar and upperworld crime is a greater danger than street crime, and, by implication, attention should be turned to the truly dangerous elements of American society, who occupy the highest seats of power in the political, economic, and military arenas. This, however, is a naive and simplistic view.

Of course white collar crime constitutes a danger to the social body. It defrauds the poor who can least afford the losses, erodes public confidence in any semblance of social morality, accounts for far more theft (in terms of millions of dollars) than all street crime could possibly do, results in more illegal arms sales than all underworld figures put together, and so one could continue.

In fact, the very term "white collar crime" has lost its meaning. Originally, when white collar referred to executives and officials, white collar crime called attention to illegal activity at the top of the social and business pyramid. But now, with many office workers in white collar occupations, and with the growing problem of employees' thefts, business executives have twisted the term to mean almost exclusively "crime by lower level employees" against the company, or government agency, for which they work. "Crime in the suites"—the executive suites which are the citadels of power—more accurately reflects the seriousness and pervasiveness with which laws are broken, so often with impunity, by the wealthy, the powerful, and the privileged.

But between crime in the suites and crime in the streets, there are dangers in the latter that should not be overlooked. As we walk from our homes to the subways, as we shop for necessities or go for a stroll to enjoy the sunshine, the upperworld crime will be taking pennies from our pockets and wallets, and will be polluting our air while protected from prosecution—but the street crime is more frightening because of its immediacy, the physical dangers of the confrontations, and the trauma resulting therefrom.

Perhaps what we need is a greater realization of the unity of crime, its derivation from a single moral ambience (or the lack of such) and a single social structure. The structure of society generates crime, but crime generates crime as well, in a manner that can be depicted as circular more than additive, for if it were additive and dynamic it would grow endlessly, or at least until, in dialectic fashion, the growth had created its strengthened antithesis, social control and social repression. The circularity of crime is illustrated by the New York scene when the city, within a period of a few months, was hit by a blackout and then by a paralyzing snowstorm. During the blackout there was widespread looting, and the same occurred when the storm came. However, the looting during the snowstorm was not called that: it was known as price gouging. Suddenly, with people unable to move more than a block or two from their homes, with many stores closed because employees or store owners could not find a way to reach them, with deliveries to such stores at a standstill or nearly so, those merchants who remained open raised their prices on milk, bread, and other necessities to as high as the market would bear. It was illegal, but there were no arrests, no outcries by an enraged public, no mayor coming on television to denounce these "animals" and promise that they would be vigorously prosecuted and not allowed to plea bargain. The looting by the store owners did not find its way into crime statistics, for police officers, if they received complaints at all, might have felt that the complainants were lucky to be able to purchase anything under such conditions.

We stop to narrate this not to prove that white collar crime is underpublicized, its importance in the effects on the lives of all of us underplayed, its perpetrators protected by a power structure whether on a communitywide or national basis, but to illustrate that even when it exists on a crass level of stealing from the mouths of the hungry, it has a different character than street crime. However, what appears to be indicated, but not sufficiently studied, is how the two types, and other types, of crime stem from similar sources; how the feeling of being victimized erodes the resistance to becoming a victimizer; and how a few persons—the criminals, ordinary criminals, who constitute only a small part of the population in their class, sex, race, ethnic group, occupation, or whatever—can be affected by the seemingly surrounding immorality and criminality, and can interpret crime as something that everyone is doing, from the highest levels down.

ANTIHUMANISTS ON THE OFFENSIVE

The antihumanists are on the offensive. That their ideology is timeworn and was discarded for its failures as well as for its affront to human dignity does not seem to phase them. The conservatives have, in the view of Walter Miller (1973), made some basic assumptions and embraced some crusading issues, as have those on the left.

To summarize and paraphrase Miller, the conservatives assume the need for a single strong moral order, security for the central position of the family as the building block in society, the need to maintain class distinctions and differences in sex roles and racial, ethnic, and religions identities, to which one can add the assumption of individual responsibility, including free will and accountability, although the latter is a cornerstone of left-leaning existentialists as well. The crusading issues of the political conservatives include the charge that excessive leniency is shown to lawbreakers, that the rights of criminals are favored over the welfare of their victims and of law enforcement personnel, that an erosion of discipline and respect for authority continues, and that permissiveness in other areas of life leads to crime.

Against this, Miller identifies the assumptions and crusading issues of the left. The assumptions are that the primary cause for criminal behavior can be located in the social system and the conditions it generates, rather than in deviant individuals and in their minds or bodies; that injustice and inequality are the root causes of dissent, rebellion that is distorted by some into criminal channels, and of general demoralization. The crusading issues—although one must add that there is diminished enthusiasm and support for them in the fading years of the decade of the seventies—continue to be the problem of overcriminalization that can at least partially be remedied by decriminalization, the burden of stigmatization and negative labeling, the overinstitutionalization of the criminal justice system, the need for deinstitutionalization and of alternatives to incarceration, and discriminatory bias that pervades the criminal justice system to the disadvantage of racial and political minorities.

This appears to us to be a well-balanced, value-free description of a confrontation of ideologies, and one that leads us to believe that a humanistic approach, embodying much of what Miller describes and no doubt correctly attributes to the left, is as viable as ever.

A prominent philosopher, and one whose record on civil rights and human freedom cannot be faulted, is reported to have indicated that the thief on the street is a greater threat to his freedom and liberty than is the police officer who may stop to frisk him or federal officials who may enter his premises without a properly documented search warrant. It is a widespread plaint, and we even suspect that many who agree fear so to state, lest they feel themselves alienated from an abiding faith with which they have lived for years, if not decades. Yet it is precisely in a situation like the present that we can affirm the propriety of the great decisions of the Warren Court, and a few that were antecedent to it, in the nationalization of the Bill of Rights and in the extension of many of its guarantees to state and not merely to federal matters.

The struggle for the nationalization of the Bill of Rights was a hard-fought one, and it is not yet over. For a century after Chief Justice Marshall interpreted the Bill of Rights as applying only to federal and not state jurisdictions, thus exempting states from requiring that there should be no double jeopardy, no cruel and unusual punishment, no freedom from forced self-incrimination (unless state constitutions so provided, as in some instances they did), the Bill of Rights was virtually nonexistent as a weapon for the protection of American liberties and for the defense of the accused. Only one decision is on record, prior to the Civil War, in which the Bill of Rights was invoked successfully in a state rather than a federal matter, and it is an irony that few will miss that this was to uphold the slaveowner in the case of Dred Scott.

First there was Scottsboro, in which the justices of the Supreme Court discovered that the "due process" clause in the Fourteenth Amendment, which had been part of the Constitution for well over half a century, meant that a defendant in a state action had certain protections under the Bill of Rights, for without them he was being deprived without due process of law of guarantees given to all Americans. Later, there was the Warren Court, and the names of the key cases are almost household words: Miranda, Escobedo, Mapp, and others. Today, the thrust of the Warren court, in extending the rights of the accused, is under greater attack. Echoing the thought if not the words of our civil-libertarian philosopher, more people believe that they are threatened by the criminals than by criminal justice agents operating without constitutional restraints. We suggest that the philosopher may be right, at least in the short run: the criminal on the street is the greater threat *to him*. But we are not at all sure that this is true of the black and other racial minorities, of lower-class people and those without the philosopher's education, articulate abilities, and associations, of youth whose lifestyles are sometimes at variance with those around them, and of such disadvantaged people as welfare recipients, antiwar and other demonstrators, homosexuals, the politically unorthodox, prostitutes, and numerous others.

Some of the new realists and all the traditional hardliners find common cause in the old refrain that "criminals are being coddled." It is said that the police are handcuffed largely by rules and restrictions imposed by "liberal professional administrators" and "timid politicians" who are more concerned with the rights of criminals than with catching and locking up the troublemakers. Leaning on the decisions of the Warren Court (or on the Bill of Rights and the U.S. Constitution, in which so many people seem to have lost faith), it is charged that clever lawyers find procedural loopholes and technicalities to obtain freedom for defendants, despite airtight cases against them. In the landmark cases before the Warren Court the defendants were not angels, but had the Constitution not applied to them what expectations might we have that it would be applied to others who are caught up in the web of an intricate judicial and prosecutorial system? False confessions are not exactly unknown in American criminal history, nor entrapment, nor cruel and unusual punishment. This, a time of real concern for safety, is not a moment for the abandonment of the Constitution to be discarded as a noble experiment, but for its reaffirmation as more necessary than ever, more of a valued instrument in a world of shrinking liberties from government leviathans armed with computers, with electronic bugging devices, and cameras with telescopic lenses that see in the dark, all beyond the imagination of an Orwell who was writing only a few years ago.

ON THE PROBLEM OF SENTENCING

There is considerable debate on indeterminate versus determinate sentences, and with it on the value of parole. Since 1870, legislatures have set minimum and maximum terms for sentences. Judges sentence convicts to "terms prescribed by law." From that time on, the prisoner falls under the jurisdiction of the parole board. The duration of individual terms is ostensibly determined by a prisoner's record: there are written reports from correctional officers that deal with such matters as chapel attendance, work accomplishments, educational achievements, assessments of attitudes by social workers and other professionals, and the outlook for that vague factor known as rehabilitation.

At one time, the indeterminate sentence was hailed as a step forward both by humanistically inclined reformers and by hardliners. For the former, it appeared that individualized treatment was necessary and humane, for it elevated the man in the dock to the position of a human being not devoid of hope. For the conservative and the punitive, it was a manner of maintaining prisoners behind bars for longer than average terms. Although statistically the conservatives have proven correct, for inmates are indeed incarcerated longer for the same offenses in states that have indeterminate than those that practice flat time, there is a general disillusionment with the whole idea of the indeterminate sentence.

Liberal reformers supported the conversion to indeterminate sentences in the hope that it would protect some prisoners from vindictive judges in enraged communities. Looking backward, it may appear naive that people at one time wished to place the fate of prisoners in the hands of more dispassionate and ostensibly professionalized experts who served on parole boards or as advisors to such bodies. Each prisoner could be watched and studied individually, and would be released when a demonstration had been shown of readiness to return to the community. Presumably, this would often be long before flat time sentences had expired, although in practice inmates were often compelled to serve for longer terms than would otherwise have been the case.

Prisoner organizations and spokesmen claim that indeterminacy has become a punitive weapon of inscrutable parole boards, petty authoritarian guards, and often of practitioners of racial discrimination. Prisoners become anxious and angry because they are unsure of the duration of their confinement. Inordinately long sentences have been served for offenses which, had the convicted individual originally been sentenced to such a stretch of time, would have aroused the concern and anguish of people throughout the world. But because the original sentence was couched in such language as "one day to life," it effectively concealed the reality of its own harshness.

It is not because the indeterminate sentences are short and the offenders are quickly back on the street that such practices are better abandoned, nor is it because indeterminate sentences do not permit those who hold the keys in the name of society to throw them away (whatever that may mean), but because there is built into the indeterminate sentence an inherent gravitational pull toward injustice. Far too much discretion is placed in the hands of people whose competence to make these determinations is limited, whose familiarity with the facts is less than complete, and who become influenced by differential social class, race, education, family background, and job opportunity considerations that further burden the already handicapped.

Justice is depicted as being blind, meaning of course that she does not see the origins and race and other irrelevant characteristics of the accused, but sees only the act itself in order to determine what it was and who was its perpetrator. Alas, blindness seems to have taken on another meaning: justice stands blind to the social realities of invidious distinctions from which some people who come before her suffer, and by contrast others benefit.

Prisoners everywhere are voicing complaints about the wide divergence of sentences meted out to people for committing very similar crimes. While no two sets of circumstances are identical, when one considers the enormity of the act, the harm done to others, whether it is a first or a second offense, and other facts, one still encounters sentence disparity that might be narrowed if discretion on the part of judges were also reduced. Race and ethnicity appear to be related to severity of sentence, and the American Civil Liberties Union has documented the fact that blacks serve longer sentences than whites, when all other factors concerning the crime and the offender are held constant. The situation becomes complex, for more recent studies have focused on the victim, and have demonstrated that offenders against black victims are treated with greater leniency than offenders against whites. That flat sentencing can likewise be a device to aid the privileged, who are more likely to be found not guilty when prison is an inevitable alternative, is another complicating factor, but hardly seems to outweigh the inequalities arising from indeterminacy.

It is not only in the sentence, but in the prison itself, that the call for reform should not be drowned out by the new fear of crime. Perhaps brutalization, dehumanization, emasculation will gratify the lust for vengeance of people who have been victimized and by their communities that live in constant fear. But it is a vicious system that will serve to brutalize not only the offenders but the victims, the members of the society who acquiesce in such inhuman treatment. It is no more realistic to speak of tearing down the walls than it is to talk of throwing away the keys, but while the walls are up and incarceration is a fact of life, it can be no less effective, whether as incapacitating or as deterring, when the inmate is shown the understanding and consideration that he failed to show to others. If this does not work toward rehabilitation it need not be abandoned, because the end in sight is more than just a deescalation of hostility, but the reduction of brutality, cruelty, and violence for its own sake, the positive affirmation of human values thus becoming a goal toward which we strive, and not merely the means of reaching some other goal.

THE RISE OF CRIME
AND THE DECLINE OF THEORY

The history of American criminology is the story of competing theories, sometimes encouraging one another in successive periods, often promulgated more or less simultaneously. If to some the theories appeared to be mutually exclusive, to others they were complementary, or at least capable of some synthesis. In a spirit of realistic modesty, here and there a theorist made more limited claims, recognizing that his view was capable of explaining less than all criminality. To mention a few is to indicate the plethora of explanations that have held sway, at least among an important sector of criminologists, over the last fifty years: ecology, differential association, body type, biological predisposition, psychoanalysis, culture conflict, general conflict (in several different theoretical forms), anomie, subculture of violence, and one might add labeling, for despite many indications that it is a perspective or an emphasis and not an explanatory tool, it does seek to explain some crime as manifestations of secondary deviance, as Carol Warren (1973) has noted.

While it would appear useful, and even predictable in the light of the history of science and the history of ideas, that there should be a period of adjustment, review, and recapitulation, reassessment, revision, synthesis, with discarding or acceptance of much of the old, following so many clashes of approaches in so short a period, we are struck by the lack of new theory during the time of greatest crime increase. Or, stated differently, by the failure of explanation for the extraordinary fluctuations in crime and for the rise that has been experienced during the 1960s and 1970s. If theory is to explain a phenomenon, it should explain its absence as well as its presence, its decline as well as its growth. What evidence is there, for example, that there has been a greater amount of differential association, or of a conflict of conduct norms, during the years of highest crime rates? It is not to deny the possibility, and the new evidence, of a biological or constitutional predisposition to crime, when one points out that the predilection, capacity, or potential must have been present to approximately the same extent in the gene pool of the people of America in its period of lower crime rates and lesser violence.

Those who have found only a vacuum, whether of new theories or of old ones that might be usable to explain new

forms and new manifestations of crime, have turned away
from theory entirely. They have renounced explanation, and
with it social change that would diminish the causes of crime,
in favor of a punitive and repressive response to the criminal.
And although many speak of society as an abstraction that is
an entity unto itself, proponents of various theories are more
successful in explaining crime in terms of society than explaining changing crime rates in terms of changing characteristics
of society. The exception, and we find it less than convincing,
is that crime is tied in with one overarching demographic
variable: the percentage of people in the age group (approximately 16 or 17 to 29 or thereabouts) who are most crime-
prone. Some have even gone so far as to suggest that if only
we can survive the next few years, crime will diminish as the
bulging curve representing the postwar baby boom matures
into its quiescent thirties.

It is entirely speculative, and perhaps ours is a period for
speculative reflection, but it appears to us that the two great
events that might have brought a larger than ever minority of
the American people to the world of crime have been the
disillusionment following the great wave of hope in the civil
rights movement, and the glorification of violence as well as
the tearing asunder of any semblance of respect for the prevailing moral order in the society when the world's first live
televised war reached into the homes of millions of Americans.

Of the first, one has only to refer to the great theoretical
works of Marx, de Tocqueville, and others to note the evidence
that resentment, rebellion, and revolt occur not when the
conditions of the masses are at a nadir, but when they have
risen slightly, when there is widespread hope, when goals seem
to be within reach, and when they slip elusively from one's
grasp. The young people in America, as well as many older
persons, were in a state not only of ferment in the 1960s, but
of expectations and dreams, of which civil rights became the
most visible and most idealized goals. While some colleges
have become integrated, as have trains and washrooms, the

ghettoization of masses of blacks and Hispanics is as severe as ever, their exploitation in no way alleviated by the fact that the favored few among them now can make it. The stark contrast of burned-out slums, hovels that pass for homes, gouging storekeepers and exploitative absentee landlords, with the hopes and expectations of yesteryear, have turned a few voices of anger to a life of crime. In the absence not only of a strong civil rights movement directed toward affecting change, some people express their resentments in the form of violence and crime. That their victims are so often the poor like themselves does not stay their hands. This is not to deny that social control in the form of police forces and deterrent and incapacitating actions are necessary, but it is doomed to become one more example for those who proclaim that "nothing works."

And Vietnam! How cavalier of the criminologists to be discussing America in the 1970s and never remember the crisis through which we passed and the scars that will be with us for many years. The subculture of violence became only a reflection of the culture of violence. This was the body-count war, the scorecard war, where victory was measured in the number of dead, of either sex, of any age, that advisors and soldiers were able to inflict on a far-off people. It is a challenge to common sense and to credulity to state that the war that came to us each day and night on television had no effect on a greater acceptance of violence as an answer to the needs of some people. A few of those persons turned to murder, rape, assault; many more to anger and incivility, whether in the streets, in schools, on public highways, and even within their homes.

WHERE DO WE GO FROM HERE?

We suggest that the necessary response to crime is justice. It means justice in the precinct house and in the courtroom for the victim and for the accused, equal justice in sentencing (including for corporate and upperworld criminals), justice in the form of humane treatment for those who are to be incarcerated. It means social justice—resocialization, destigmatization, social acceptance, and with it good housing and good jobs—for those released from prison.

A society will not reduce crime until it ceases creating new cohorts of criminals from the ranks of those it has oppressed, rejected, and discarded. These people, or at least the young who are growing into their ranks, can be infused with hope and confidence in the world around them. The lesson seems too obvious to need restating: a society that has social rejects will suffer from their depredations.

REFERENCES

GOULDNER, A. W. (1970) The Coming Crisis of Western Sociology. New York: Basic Books.

MERTON, R. K. (1976) Sociological Ambivalence and Other Essays. New York: Free Press.

MILLER, W. B. (1973) "Ideology and criminal justice policy: some current issues." J. of Criminal Law and Criminology 64: 141-162.

WARREN, C.A.B. (1976) "Labeling theory: the individual, the category and the group." Paper presented to Society for Study of Social Problems, New York. [Cited by D. Glaser (1978) "Deviance, crime, alienation, and anomie," in E. Sagarin (ed.) Sociology: The Basic Concepts. New York: Holt, Rinehart & Winston.].

12

CORPORATE CRIME
Issues in Research

MARSHALL B. CLINARD
PETER C. YEAGER
University of Wisconsin—Madison

after many vicissitudes, the issue of corporate crime has at last become a real concern to the public, government, and criminologists. Opinion polls have shown that increasingly large proportions of the public have grave doubts about the honesty and integrity of major corporations in the United States (Walton, 1977: vii). Many federal regulatory agencies, including the Securities and Exchange Commission, Federal Trade Comission, Food and Drug Administration, Environmental Protection Agency, and others, as well as corresponding state agencies, have become more and more active in prosecuting the illegal behavior of large corporations, a trend indicated both in agencies' annual reports and in the increasing numbers of accounts printed in such major periodicals as the *Wall Street Journal.* In addition, while monetary penalties for corporate violations were minimal until relatively recently, Congress has significantly increased the penalties in a number of areas; for instance, the Federal Water Pollution Control Act provides for civil penalties of up to $10,000 per day, and criminal fines of up to $25,000 per day of the violation (up to $50,000 for second convictions). That these penalties can mount up precipitously was demonstrated in 1976 when Allied Chemical Corporation was fined several million dollars in connection with discharges of the pesticide Kepone into Virginia's James River. Furthermore, the Department of

Justice has been demanding ever stronger penalties. In one 1978 price-fixing case, for example, nine executives of various corporations were imprisoned (sentences of one or three months), more sentences issued in this case than was customary in past cases (*Wall Street Journal,* 1978: 11). In such price-fixing cases, fines of up to $1 million for the corporation and $100,000 for individuals can be imposed. The proposed Federal Criminal Code provides for general corporate penalties of up to $500,000. Some persons still maintain that these fines are not sufficiently severe in relation to the ill-gotten gains from corporate violations. However, corporations often lack ready cash and penalties often reduce profits. In addition, the possible widespread adverse publicity may seriously reduce the public's confidence in the corporation and thus benefit its competition.

It is generally agreed that the first empirical study to convince criminologists of the importance of research in this field was carried out by Sutherland (1949). His *White Collar Crime* dealt with the illegal behavior of 70 of the 200 largest U.S. non-financial corporations. Somewhat later Mannheim (1965: 470) suggested that if there were to be a Nobel Prize for criminology, certainly Sutherland would have been the foremost candidate for his work on white collar and corporate crime. During the 25 years following Sutherland's provocative work, however, there was little follow-up research, with only minimal study being carried out on illegal corporate behavior. Some articles and books have appeared, but most of them have been either of a rather general nature or limited to a few case studies, primarily of anitrust violations in the electrical industry or of selected regulatory agencies (cf. Geis, 1967; Turner, 1970). Only a relatively few quantitative research articles have appeared, and these have been narrow in scope, again dealing largely with antitrust violations (cf. Burton, 1966). This relative lack of research is significant; Sutherland's study is still the primary research on corporate crime. Thus, it continues to be widely cited, despite the facts that the

data are old, the study is no longer relevant, the methodological procedures were weak, and little systematic attempt
was made to analyze the data with the use of independent
variables. Furthermore, the study covered only federal law
violations by a small group of large corporations.

Although criminologists previously had paid lip service to
the topic, largely it has been only since the mid-1970s that they
have incorporated the area of corporate crime into the discipline and have begun to study it seriously. Probably the
first basic book to include a chapter on corporate crime
appeared in 1973 (Clinard and Quinney, 1973: ch. 8). Today
textbooks conventionally include a chapter or lengthy discussion of this subject. Corporate crime first appeared as a
separate topic at a professional society meeting at the 1975
session of the American Society of Criminology; in each subsequent year there has been a section on corporate crime, and
such sections are now included in the meetings of the Society
for the Study of Social Problems and the American Sociological Association. Articles on corporate crime are appearing
more frequently in professional journals. Although only a few
empirical investigations are currently underway, the interest is
now substantial and research will undoubtedly increase
rapidly.

REASONS FOR THE DEARTH OF RESEARCH

Many factors might be cited in explaining the paucity of
research efforts involving corporate illegalities. One of the
barriers to criminological research in this area is simply lack
of experience and appropriate training. For criminologists
trained in criminal law and accustomed to studying individual
offenders, the study of corporate crime necessitates a significant retooling, involving familiarity with the concepts and
research in the areas of political sociology, complex organizations, administrative law (e.g., the regulatory agencies), civil

law, and economics. Corporate violations and their control occur in a complex political and economic environment, and most often involve administrative and civil sanctions to which criminologists generally have had limited exposure. Furthermore, most enforcement is carried out by state and federal regulatory agencies rather than by the courts, and criminologists have had little experience with such organizations. In the past, it was generally believed difficult to gain access to the enforcement data of regulatory agencies or court cases that involve corportions. Finally, limited funds have been available for research in this area, while resources have been plentiful for studies of ordinary crime, due partly to a lack of concern for research on illegal corporate behavior and partly to the fact that criminologists have felt unable to set up viable research projects. As a result, many criminologists have taken the easy path and continued to study conventional crime or, at best, small-scale consumer frauds.

SOCIAL FORCES AND
THE RECOGNITION OF CORPORATE CRIME

The growing recognition of corporate crime as an area for criminological research has largely been a natural response to various social forces. Particularly important has been the growth in public concern about corporate wrongdoings. Historically in the United States, major public concern has shifted from one type of crime to another, concentrating in turn on such areas as organized crime, "street crime," drug peddling, rape, and child abuse. Such changing concerns have greatly influenced how legislators and government enforcement agencies act with regard to certain behaviors, and have even influenced criminologists' choice of research topics.

In general terms, perhaps the central development promoting the growth of public and criminological concern with business crime has simply been the dramatic increase in the role and impact of major corporations in contemporary American society. Corporations such as Exxon, General Motors, IBM, and ITT are giant aggregations of wealth and political and social power, and their operations vitally influence the lives of virtually everyone "from the cradle to the grave."[1] The major corporations control the worklives—and hence the health and safety—of much of the population; have massive effects on prices (and therefore inflation), the quality of goods, and the unemployment rate; can manipulate public opinion through the use of mass media; palpably affect the environment and foreign relations; and, as the disclosures of recent years suggest, can jeopardize the democratic process with illegal political contributions. As Ralph Nader (1973: 79) noted—with only a touch of hyperbole—in connection with the difficulties, "Our states are no match for the resources and size of our great corporations; General Motors could *buy* Delaware . . . if DuPont were willing to sell it." The major corporations are the central institutions in our society. Little wonder that public and regulatory attention has turned increasingly toward them.

It is possible to identify some of the more specific social forces in American society which have contributed to what appears to be an almost sudden criminological interest and concern with corporate crime. They include certain highly publicized corporate violations, corporate irresponsibility and the growth of the consumer movement, increased environmental concern, reaction to the overconcentration on concern with lower class crimes and poverty problems, the black revolution and the prison reform movement, and the influence of conflict analysis and radical criminology.

1. The electrical conspiracy of the 1960s that involved most of the major electrical corporations in a highly secret and devious price-fixing operation received little publicity in the mass media (Dershowitz, 1961), even though it probably resulted in a greater loss than all burglaries committed during a single year (President's Commission on Law Enforcement

and Administration of Justice, 1967: 48). On the other hand, in recent years widespread publicity has been given to the Watergate crimes and the illegal political contributions by over 300 large corporations to the Nixon campaign, to the highly publicized role of ITT in heading off antitrust actions by a large contribution to the Republican National Convention, the political contribution of the Associated Milk Producers to obtain an increase in milk price supports, and the flagrant violations of the huge Equity Funding Corporation with its enormous losses. These cases particularly have led to the growth of public concern and increasing negative attitudes toward corporations, as shown in public opinion polls. In addition, many illegal actions of large corporations are being shifted to the front pages of daily newspapers from the less obvious financial pages. Now a few of these cases have even received wide publicity on nationally televised news broadcasts.

2. The widespread consumer movements were officially launched during the late 1960s with Ralph Nader's protest that the General Motors automobile, the Corvair, was "unsafe at any speed," and they were advanced by the subsequent research and widespread dissemination of over 50 studies done by Nader's group in other corporate areas. In recent years numerous consumer agencies have been created at federal and state levels, and laws designed to protect the buyer have resulted in greater liability of manufacturers for their widely distributed products. It has been estimated that by 1978 the federal government alone is annually receiving 10 million consumer complaints (Mouat, 1978). As a result of these public concerns various proposals have been presented for more drastic curbs on corporate power (Nader et al., 1972; Stone, 1975).

3. The growth of concern with the abuses to the environment culminated in the creation of the federal Environmental Protection Agency and numerous state and local level counterparts. Since corporations have been found to be major vio-

lators, widespread publicity has been given to cases of corporate air and water pollution, the use of harmful chemicals in manufacturing processes, and to other abuses of the natural environment.

4. During the 1960s governmental and private efforts were directed at the eradication of poverty, on the assumption that poverty was a necessary and sufficient condition for the commission of crimes. This overconcentration on poverty itself as an explanation of crime highlighted the inappropriateness of the application of this frame of reference to the unethical and illegal behavior of white collar groups and corporations.

5. Likewise during the 1960s, the black revolution and the prison reform movement called attention indirectly to the disproportionate representation of both blacks and poor in our prisons. Informed persons began asking what happened to the middle and upper class persons and the corporate executives who violated the law. The short sentences of a few months, or suspended sentences, given to Watergate offenders and to corporate offenders heightened the contrast between this leniency and the 10, 20, and even 50-year sentences given for burglary and robbery offenses. Today the threat of a criminal penalty against corporate executives is becoming a major governmental tool in the control of corporate violations.

6. Finally, the more static structural-functional approach to society taken by social scientists such as Talcott Parsons has been increasingly challenged by a Marxist or neo-Marxist interpretation in terms of class conflict. This approach has spread into the discipline as the radical or the new criminology, and has resulted in numerous publications, including those by Quinney, Chambliss, and Ian Taylor. Most of these works have pointed out the role of corporate abuses of power in a capitalist society and the relative immunity of the corporations from prosecution and penalties, particularly as compared to the lower and working class groups. Although their positions have often been overstated, they have had a salutary

effect in making criminologists question whether they have been class-biased in their research and other work. Criminologists have become aware that they have perhaps contributed to the public image of "the criminal" as a lower class person who commits the conventional crimes of larceny and burglary rather than the crimes of the corporate suites.

CORPORATE ETHICS AND LAW VIOLATIONS

A corporation exists to make profits; stockholders own stocks in a corporation with that same expectation. Social irresponsibility and unethical practices can flourish in such a setting. Unethical practices in turn set the stage for violations of law, as the practices within corporate settings often tend eventually to conflict with those values imposed by law (Quinney, 1964). Two anonymous surveys by large corporations of their managers, and those of other corporations, found that management feels under pressure to compromise personal ethics in order to achieve corporate goals. For example, "most managers believed that their peers would not refuse orders to market off-standard and possibly dangerous products" (Madden, 1977: 67; the surveys were commissioned by Pitney-Bowes Inc. and Uniroyal Corporation). This unethical behavior is justified primarily by the beliefs that if one has had good intentions one has behaved ethically, that what is workable is good, and that the marketing ethic is giving the customers what they want (Walton, 1977: 8-9). Corporate loyalty, carrying out the orders of someone else in management, and the desire to get ahead in salaries and bonuses are further justifications.

Ethical violations are of many types and are closely linked to corporate crime. (1) Exaggerated claims and misrepresentation of products have long been common sales practices. Advertising which is not necessarily illegal, but which is misleading, is widespread in newspapers, magazines, billboards, and on television. These practices have been termed advertising "puffing," such as "Ford gives you better ideas," "Breakfast of Champions," and "You can be sure if it's Westinghouse" (Preston, 1975). It is extremely difficult to distinguish "puffery" from illegal deception (Kintner, 1971). (2) The representation in the advertising media, particularly television, that the corporation is socially responsible and primarily interested in the general welfare instead of maximum profits, gives a false or "political" image and is unethical. (3) Harmful and unsafe products are frequently produced in the manufacture of autos, tires, appliances, children's toys, cosmetics, and drugs, and they are merchandised on the grounds that others are involved in selling such products or that it is an acceptable means of making a profit if the government does not make such production illegal. (4) Often virtually worthless products, such as foods and drugs—food items that lack nutritional qualities or over-the-counter drugs whose claimed effects have not been demonstrated—are marketed with assertions of their great values. Of the $780 billion spent by consumers in 1969, Senator Philip Hart estimated that about $200 billion had been expended on products of no value. (5) Manufacturers commonly refrain from developing or manufacturing cheaper products, withhold more efficient products from the market, or build obsolescence into their products. (6) Where there are no legal prohibitions, the physical environment is often disregarded and the country's natural resources exploited without adequate regard to either the resulting harmful effects or its possible effects on future generations. (7) The kickbacks or "gifts" given to purchasing agents are common practices which are only slightly different from pay-offs or the actual bribery of purchasers or officials, domestic or foreign. (8) Competitors are frequently spied upon, or their employees hired away from companies, in order to learn business secrets. (9) The possibility of future corporate employment is held open to employees of government agencies involved in regulating corporations. (10) Many corporations are operated to gain personal benefits for corporate management at the expense of the stockholders and the government, including expensive executive "perks." (11) Among further violations of ethics may be included the invasion of the privacy of employees, the firing of employees after years of service to save profits, and the lack of social responsibility to the community in which a corporation is operating.

Only a short step separates these unethical tactics from actual violations of the law. Many corporate practices which were formerly considered only unethical have now been made illegal and punished by government. Consequently, corporate crime today includes tax evasion such as false inventory values for tax purposes; unfair labor practices involving union rights, minimum wage regulations, working conditions, and overtime; violations of safety regulations concerning, for example, occupational safety and health; price-fixing to stabilize market prices and to eliminate competition; food and drug law violations; air and water pollution in violation of governmental standards; violation of energy regulations including rules on energy conservation; submission of false information for the sale of securities; false advertising and illegal rebates. It is doubtful that these practices would be approved by stockholders. Stone (1975: 82) has written as follows about such practices: "Even if management *had* made an express promise to its shareholders to 'maximize your profits' I am not persuaded that the ordinary person would interpret it to mean 'maximize *in every way you can possibly get away with,* even if that means polluting the environment, ignoring and breaking the law.' "

DIFFICULTIES IN
RESEARCHING CORPORATE CRIME

The first large-scale empirical study of corporate crime since Sutherland's work in 1949 is now being carried out by the authors and a research staff.[2] It involves a systematic analysis of federal and state actions (administrative, civil, and criminal) taken against the 624 largest U.S. corporations—industrial, wholesale, retail, and service—and their subsidiaries during 1975 and 1976. The difficulties encountered in this research partially explain the paucity of studies in the area of corporate crime, as well as the types of problems which should be anticipated by those who plan such research.

COMPLEXITY OF CORPORATIONS

The study of corporate wrongdoing cannot be likened to the investigation of burglars, embezzlers, or occupational criminals such as unscrupulous doctors who bilk welfare programs. Corporate crime is *organizational* crime which occurs in the context of complex and varied sets of structured relationships between boards of directors, executives, managers, and other employees on the one hand, and between parent corporation, corporate divisions, and subsidiaries on the other. Even with increased familiarity with the subtleties and varieties of corporate structure, the analyst working in this area will still face methodological difficulties stemming from the organizational nature of corporate phenomena. For instance, one sort of analytical problem which often arises is the difficulty in legally determining exactly where, and by whom, in the corporate structure the decision to violate has been made. For those interested in studying the *processes* underlying illegal corporate behavior, this problem requires carefully done qualitative investigations of selected cases. Such research involves the study of administrative agency and court documents and transcripts, as well as (ideally) interviews with regulatory and corporate personnel involved in the case.

Corporate complexity provides other methodological challenges to the quantitative researcher interested in the structural and economic correlates of business crime. One such problem is product diversification. Many corporations are huge conglomerates with annual sales that often total in the billions of dollars, and which are derived from a number of varied product lines. While such corporations may have a "main line" of business, they derive significant portions of their income from activities quite remote from their central product. For instance, International Telephone & Telegraph owns the Sheraton Hotel Corporation as well as business concerns in a variety of other fields, while Greyhound, noted nationally for its bus service, owns Armour and Company, a major meatpacker. Consequently, the researcher desiring to study violations by type of industry faces classification difficulties. One may choose to classify corporations by primary industry as assigned by investor's services. However, in this era of growing diversification and merger, some such classification may not be unambiguous, and the researcher should be aware of any limitations of its use for the corporate sample being analyzed.

Finally, the question of corporate subsidiaries can prove troublesome. Large corporations often have many subsidiaries in numerous product lines; in fact, in our sample we estimate that the 624 parent corporations own in the neighborhood of 9000 subsidiaries, 110 of which have annual sales of $300 million (the lowest figure in our corporation sample) or more, and 28 of which sell more than a billion dollars worth annually. In the attempt to compile the violations records of corporations, one would ideally include all violations of all subsidiaries. In a study the size we have undertaken, this is not practical, especially since violations of subsidiaries are often not reported with the name of the parent corporation. Consequently, we have chosen to focus on tnose wholly owned subsidiaries with at least $300 million in annual sales.

DATA DIFFICULTIES

Despite the severe limitations of the *Uniform Crime Reports*, there exists no equivalent report for the study of corporate crime. For the foreseeable future, the researcher himself must gather the data. Obviously, an equivalent of crimes reported to the police is not possible, except perhaps in the area of consumer complaints. In addition, investigations of corporations undertaken by authorities are difficult to obtain in many cases, simply because the records are often not publicly available unless violations have been revealed. Generally, the researcher must deal with enforcement actions initiated against companies (roughly the equivalent of arrests or prosecutions) and actions completed (equivalent to convictions). Such data are not easily available for studies such as ours. In order to compensate for deficiencies in completeness and comprehensiveness in any one source, we are relying on four main sources of data, some of which would not have been publicly available prior to the Freedom of Information Act of 1974:

(1) Data obtained directly from federal agencies on enforcement actions taken against the corporations in our sample.

(2) Law service reports (principally those of Commerce Clearing House and the Bureau of National Affairs) which give decisions involving corporation cases in such areas as antitrust, consumer product safety, and environmental pollution.

(3) Annual corporation financial reports (Forms 10-K) prepared for the SEC, which include a section on legal proceedings initiated against the firms.

(4) A computer printout of abstracts of enforcement proceedings involving corporations which have been reported in the *New York Times, The Wall Street Journal* and the leading trade journals.

In our attempt to study comprehensively the violations policed by more than 25 federal agencies and numerous state agencies, it is obviously not reasonable to expect a complete data set. First, government data on corporate violations vary in accessibility; some agency data are readily available on computers or through printed materials, while other data are kept only by date or case number or are available only in regional or district offices. Furthermore, data are generally kept in forms more useful for agency operational use than for outside research purposes. An example of such a situation is provided by the Department of the Interior's Mining Enforcement and Safety Administration which regulates mining safety conditions; though on computer, its approximately 90,000 cases a year covering over 15,000 mines are listed by name of mine rather than by parent corporation. Second, some violations data cannot be made public, even under the Freedom of Information Act. Such is the case for tax actions taken by the Internal Revenue Service except when, as seldom happens, the enforcement proceeding goes to appeal. Third, informal enforcement actions (as opposed to the formal administrative and judicial proceedings) are often difficult to collect as they are not always reported by district or regional agencies. Finally, the reporting of federal court cases in the *Federal Supplement* is not complete, and is left to the discretion of the individual courts.

Besides varying degrees of completeness, law service reports are somewhat difficult to use in that they are designed for the lawyer and businessman rather than for the sociologist. One practical problem which results is that the researcher must often read rather lengthy case reports to extract fundamental information on such variables as the violation, its date of occurrence, the penalty, among others. In addition, some such information may be missing from the account. Case material in 10-K reports to the SEC is also incomplete. The SEC requirement is that corporations report legal actions which may significantly affect their financial positions. With this system, minor violations can be expected to be seriously underreported. Finally, there is the problem of editorial selectivity in newspapers and other periodicals.

SANCTIONS

A major factor inhibiting research into corporate legal violations has been that criminologists' training has seldom included administrative and civil law and procedure.[3] Though the use of criminal sanctions in corporate cases is increasing, the bulk of enforcement actions are taken administratively by the many regulatory agencies. Research dealing with the enforcement behavior of numerous agencies requires knowing the natures of, and differences between, a wide range of possible sanctions, including warning letters, regulatory letters, notices of violation, administrative consent orders, court consent decrees, corrective action plans, recalls, seizures, injunctions, divestiture, class actions, contempt proceedings, and the like. Furthermore, it is necessary to be familiar with the administrative procedures of the various agencies, so that one is able to know, for example, when an administrative action has been finalized (cf. the differences between provisional and final consent orders). Moreover, each governmental agency often has its own unique set of enforcement actions and procedures, and the researcher often needs to contact the agency to clarify particulars.

SELECTED ANALYTICAL HURDLES

Research on corporate crime involves several analytical difficulties. One problem is comparing and ranking the relative seriousness of sanctions, even within a given type of sanction. The same ranking problem applies to assessing the absolute and relative seriousness of the various violations. Is a price-fixing scheme more harmful than fouling the environment or marketing untested or unsafe goods? And, within a single regulatory area (trade regulation), is an illegal merger affecting commerce in five northwestern states more serious than a false advertising campaign conducted nationally for a single product? And are strict liability offenses such as oil spills in any way comparable to corporate offenses in which individual or group blame is assessed? These are only a few of the questions with which a researcher in this area must grapple.

The seriousness question is significant in an additional direction. How many violations need a corporation tally before it is said to represent a serious crime problem? (Similarly, how much aggregate corporate criminality consititutes a national problem?) For example, Sutherland (1949) felt that his reported average of 14 government sanctions per corporation over an average period of 45 years constituted a serious corporate crime problem. However, it is difficult to make such a numerical determination of seriousness when a corporation has perhaps 50 to 100 subsidiaries, sales in the billions of dollars, a wide variety of product lines, and is subject to the control of a large number of state and federal agencies and a proliferating body of regulations, legislation, and case law.

OBJECTIVITY

A major difficulty encountered in doing research in the area of corporate crime is the maintenance of objectivity and the avoidance of moral judgments about corporate illegalities. This scientific canon is often violated by criminologists working in this field, in contrast to the field of conventional crime where the burglar, or other type of offender, is seldom morally condemned. One possible explanation for the differences in maintaining objectivity lies in the liberal political and economic views of many social scientists and criminologists who are doing such research. These views often lead to biased attitudes and research concerning corporations. In addition, social scientists are probably more sensitive than laymen to the ramifying social harm done by unethical and illegal corporate conduct.

CONCLUSIONS

This partial catalogue of problems is not meant to discourage research. Quite the contrary. Our experience indicates that while the difficulties are real, they are not only tractable but also provide stimulating challenges to the inventive analyst interested in the issue of corporate crime. Further research experience and familiarity with the data will doubt-lessly produce more refined studies, as old limitations are over-come and new barriers confronted. Furthermore, it is im-perative that criminology include this increasingly significant matter in its theoretical and applied work if sense is to be made of the "crime problem" and beginnings made toward its significant reduction. Writers in such areas as law, administra-tive science, and economics have, to a limited extent, studied corporate illegalities from the viewpoints of their respective specialties. It remains to study the nature and extent of corporate criminality and to construct integrated sociological explanations, joining such traditional criminological concerns as criteria for sanctioning and deterrence with such concepts as power and structural constraint in interorganizational relationships.

NOTES

1. The annual sales of many of the individual corporations exceed the gross national products of most nations in the world; they also surpass the general revenues of most of the states and cities in the United States (Nader, 1973: 90-93).

2. A pilot study in 1976 was supported by the University of Wisconsin—Madison Research Committee. The present study is supported by a 21-month grant (begin-ning in September, 1977) provided by the Law Enforcement Assistance Administra-tion of the U.S. Department of Justice. The senior author is the project director; the junior author is senior research assistant.

3. It is imperative that this deficiency be corrected in the academic training of graduate students in criminology.

REFERENCES

BURTON, J. F., Jr. (1966) "An economic analysis of Sherman Act criminal cases," in J. M. Clabault and J. F. Burton, Jr. (eds.) Sherman Act Indictments 1955-1965: A Legal and Economic Analysis. New York: Federal Legal Publications.

CLINARD, M. B. and R. QUINNEY (1973) "Corporate criminal behavior," ch. 8 in M. B. Clinard and R. Quinney (eds.) Criminal Behavior Systems: A Typology (rev. ed.). New York: Holt, Rinehart & Winston.

DERSHOWITZ, A. J. (1961) "Increasing community control over corporate crime—a problem in the law of sanctions." Yale Law J. 71 (December): 280-306.

GEIS, G. (1967) "White collar crime: the heavy electrical equipment anti-trust cases of 1961," pp. 139-151 in M. B. Clinard and R. Quinney (eds.) Criminal Behavior Systems: A Typology. New York: Holt, Rinehart & Winston.

KINTNER, E. W. (1971) A Primer on the Law of Deceptive Practices. New York: Macmillan.

MADDEN, C. (1977) "Forces which influence ethical behavior," pp. 31-78 in C. C. Walton (ed.) The Ethics of Corporate Conduct. Englewood Cliffs, NJ: Prentice-Hall.

MANNHEIM, H. (1965) Comparative Criminology. Boston: Houghton Mifflin.

MOUAT, L. (1978) "Consumers on the march." Christian Sci. Monitor (January 27).

NADER, R. (1973) "The case for federal chartering," pp. 67-93 in R. Nader and M. J. Green (eds.) Corporate Power in America. New York: Grossman.

——— M. J. GREEN, and J. SELIGMAN (1972) Taming the Giant Corporation. New York: Norton.

President's Commission on Law Enforcement and Administration of Justice (1967) The Challenge of Crime in a Free Society. Washington, DC: Government Printing Office.

PRESTON, I. (1975) The Great American Blow-Up: Puffery in Advertising and Selling. Madison: Univ. of Wisconsin Press.

QUINNEY, R. (1964) "The study of white collar crime: toward a reorientation in theory and research." J. of Criminal Law, Criminology and Police Sci. 55 (June): 208-214.

STONE, C. (1975) Where the Law Ends: The Social Control of Corporate Behavior. New York: Harper & Row.

SUTHERLAND, E. H. (1949) White Collar Crime. New York: Holt, Rinehart & Winston.

TURNER, J. S. (1970) The Chemical Feast. New York: Grossman.

Wall Street Journal (1978) "Stiff penalties for price-fixing levied by court." February 6.

WALTON, C. [ed.] (1977) The Ethics of Corporate Conduct. Englewood Cliffs, NJ: Prentice-Hall.

13

LOOKING BACKWARD AND FORWARD
Criminologists on Criminology as a Career

GILBERT GEIS
University of California, Irvine

ROBERT F. MEIER
Washington State University

Veteran criminologists—those whose research and teaching careers began in the 1940s and 1950s or thereabouts—have seen dramatic changes both in their discipline and in academic life in general. Criminology, housed almost exclusively in departments of sociology during the 1950s and 1960s, was (and still is) a low status sociological enterprise, grouped with such déclassé areas as marriage and the family and social problems. Only one criminologist, Edwin H. Sutherland, appears on the roster of presidents of the American Sociological Association, serving in 1939.

In the mid-1960s, a number of events took place to alter the condition of criminological work. Particularly significant was the movement in 1964 by national presidential candidates of the issue of crime control into public awareness and controversy. The perquisites for established academic criminologists flowed in abundance thereafter: federal commission positions, research funds, consulting jobs. So did the offspring of these boons: money, travel, publicity, and popular, though not necessarily academic, prestige. The wits now said that perhaps

AUTHORS' NOTE: *This is a revised version of a paper presented at the annual meeting of the American Society of Criminology, Atlanta, November 1977.*

crime doesn't pay, but criminology certainly does—and very well.

The following decade saw further significant developments. Deviance theory and theorists burst forth, nourished by an ethos that defined their concerns as less in the applied realm and therefore, by sociological standards, more exalted and significant than criminology, which traditionally has been perceived by outsiders as akin to correctional work. At the same time, criminology spawned an articulate "critical" faction, Marxist in orientation. Why criminology proved particularly hospitable to radical writings, both in the United States and, even more significantly and in a more sophisticated fashion, in Great Britain remains unclear, although the means of repression of the criminal justice system—police armaments, prisons, executions—take on more than merely symbolic qualities. Whatever the explanation, the onslaught of radicalism perhaps seriously threatened the entrenched cadre of criminologists. As Robert Merton (1957) has suggested, scholars are prone toward monomania and paranoia about their ideas—these are, after all, the only thing they have to show for their efforts—a fact, a theory, an idea, perhaps a gland (Langhan's) or a measurement (Ampère, Fahrenheit) that will make their name "immortal."[1]

David Riesman (1957) has observed that intellectual squatter's rights are particularly pronounced in social science as compared with law—both trades that Riesman followed. Without disciples, social scientists may find themselves very rapidly obsolescent paradigmatically. Howard P. Becker once noted in a graduate seminar how bitter a colleague of his had become because no one cared any longer about the work he had done on the sociology of revolutions—the subject had become passé. Becker's (1950) own ideas about the value of "sacred" and "secular" as analytical tools by means of which to describe social systems would fade away almost simultaneously with Becker's own demise. For experienced criminologists, hegemony achieved by radical criminologists could render a major share of their work anachronistic.

Scholarship, in short, can be a fickle mistress. Criminologists, buffeted since the 1950s by both fair and foul winds, offer a particularly intriguing group for study. They have failed (it seems fair to say) if their mission was to have an impact upon the amount of crime. Their earlier ideas about the handling of offenders in rehabilitative modes are in disrepute. At the same time, the subject matter is being absorbed into adjacent disciplines, such as economics and psychology, and an independent entity called "criminal justice" is gaining numerous disciplinary adherents. Forty years ago, Thorsten Sellin (1938) had noted that criminologists were intellectual nomads, persons without a disciplinary homeland.

What do veteran criminologists think of these matters? Looking back on their own careers and on the developments that have taken place during their working span, what views do they now hold about their occupational choice? What do they see ahead? If they had another chance, would they do what they did? What advice do they have to offer newcomers? These are some of the matters about which we sought information.

SAMPLE

We selected our sample from a list provided by the Center for Studies of Criminology and Criminal Law at the University of Pennsylvania of persons who had a piece of work (book or article) heavily cited in the criminological literature (excluding that on police, courts, and corrections) during the period 1945 through 1972. The cutoff point for citations was 40, with the largest number of references equaling 648, a distinction shared by Howard S. Becker's *Outsiders* (1963) and Sheldon and Eleanor Glueck's *Unraveling Juvenile Delinquency* (1950).[2]

Persons deceased (e.g., Sutherland), as well as those no longer very closely associated with the field of criminology/deviance (e.g., Redl), were eliminated from the sample. We included editors of volumes, but only the first-named author of works jointly produced. Forty-four scholars ultimately were identified in the sample;[3] from these, we received 16 usable responses. Two persons demurred from replying to the questions because, they said, they felt that they no longer were in touch with the field of criminology/deviance; two questionnaires proved undeliverable; and one person in our cohort, we were informed, was out of the country and unavailable before our deadline. The 41% response rate from "eligible" respondents was adequate for our task, since we were not seeking precise measures of the extent to which any position was held, but rather were attempting to obtain some suggestive ideas from experienced and, measured by our standard, successful workers in the field of criminology/deviance.

The kinds of scholars appearing on the list, a matter that undoubtedly will be addressed in some detail when the work of the Center at the University of Pennsylvania is completed, merit comment. All the names are readily recognizable to any criminology initiate, itself a function of the selection criterion. We suspect, though, that the ordering and even the inclusion of certain persons would be significantly different were another standard—preeminence, pathbreaking contributions, or similar (and much less readily measurable) yardsticks employed. Among other things, the number of citations to a work is a function of writing on a subject that, unlike the sociology of revolutions, remains fashionable. In addition, it tends to be true that persons who assume categoric and *outré* positions on important and respectable issues will almost routinely be attended to, if only for rebuttal purposes. Thus, from an earlier criminological generation, relatively sophisticated eclectics such as Paul Topinard vanish speedily, while scholars with a highly exaggerated emphasis on a single matter, such as Cesare Lombroso, never fail to surface in present-day discussions of criminological theory.

This is not to say, however, that our sample is notably idiosyncratic. To a large extent, most persons represented would appear on any ranking of leading contributors to the field of criminology and deviance in recent decades. It is (in terms of the present authors' standards, of course) the appearance of publications such as Frederic Wertham's *The Show of Violence,* Starke Hathaway and Elio Monachesi's *Analyzing and Predicting Juvenile Delinquency with the MMPI,* and Harry Anslinger's *Traffic in Narcotics* that makes the list an interesting piece of datum for a sociology of knowledge analysis.

FINDINGS

Healthiest developments. The ambiguous nature of the half-dozen open-ended questions that constituted our inventory was by design. We wanted respondents to feel free to find relevant any views that they might hold strongly about their personal involvement in criminology and its development as a field of study and work. Thus, we did not offer hints about what kinds of things they should regard in considering the current state of the subject's health—personnel, research, organizational, or other kinds of matters.

Two emphases clearly stood out in the answers we received about "the most healthy development in the field" during the respondents' careers. The first stressed the growing sophistication of technical skills being brought to bear upon the analysis of criminological issues. "An increasing scientificity— quantitative, empirical, multiple regression capabilities," one respondent noted, encapsulating the essence of several additional replies. Another qualified this view somewhat, saying that it was "methodological (not statistical) developments and refinements" that most impressed him.[4]

The second focus was on what the respondents perceived as a better marriage between criminological work and behavioral science theory. "This development," one respondent noted, "has been accompanied by a marked decline in the individualistic theories of psychiatry and psychology." Both deviance theory and organizational theory were stressed by one respondent as possessing revitalizing strengths for criminological research. The most articulate response in this vein is quoted below:

> The field of criminology/deviance has become less insular with respect to mainstream developments in the social and behavioral sciences over the past quarter of a century. We are still too prone to develop special theories for the phenomena we study, rather than turning to the basic disciplines for their contribution to understanding phenomena. But this is less true now.... In a sense, we are returning to the practices of an even earlier era, when mainstream sociologists were concerned with crime, and criminology and deviance were less separate fields. While specialization has led to much excellent research and imaginative theorizing, it has also tended to isolate us from mainstream developments.

There were, at the same time, a few individualistic and some iconoclastic animadversions worth note: "An increasing scepticism about the unexamined claims of liberal do-gooders" was what one respondent thought was healthiest. Two respondents believed that examination of the criminal process and societal reaction to crime were notable developments, but one took exception to what he regarded, in this vein, as "unwarranted focus" on "labeling" and "vulgarized Marxism," and another specified that he thought the "conflict" emphasis, while beneficial, was "overstated." Lastly, one respondent was heartened by what he regarded as the "fragmentation of organizations [and presumably of viewpoints] into subunits" which, he thought, made more possible "a democratic articulation of diverse viewpoints."

Influential books. We had hypothesized that works read during their formative intellectual period, such as when they were graduate students, would prove most influential for this group of scholars, though we offered them at least a slim chance to disprove our presumption by phrasing the question in the following manner: "What academic book/article made the greatest impression on you?" Presumably, it could have been something that they had read only the day before, and more certainly something they had read after they had begun their own work.

It is notable that only one article (in contrast to books) was cited by any respondent, Merton's paper on anomie which appeared in 1938. For the remainder, by far the leading responses focused on the works of Edwin H. Sutherland, notably his textbook and his *White Collar Crime* (1949), and volumes by members of the Chicago School, such as Robert Park and Ernest Burgess. The books cited by our respondents had a mean copyright date of 1947, and only two had been published in the 1970s, Marvin E. Wolfgang et al.'s *Delinquency in a Birth Cohort* (1972) and James Q. Wilson's *Thinking About Crime* (1975)—"not a great book, but at least a little heterodox," wrote our respondent. Standard classics, such as writings by Emile Durkheim, Max Weber, Karl Marx, and Talcott Parsons, were often mentioned. Strikingly, to our minds, there were no nonprofessional volumes (except a single noting of *The Bible*), such as works of literature, and only very rare notation of slightly more esoteric works, such as Michel Foucault's *Madness and Civilization* (1965) and Thomas Plint's *Crime in England* (1851).

Least healthy developments. We had thought, when we established the hypotheses that would help guide analysis of the responses we received, that there would be more agreement about healthy developments than about malaise within the field of criminology/deviance. It was our assumption that, as influential persons in criminology, the respondents would generalize from the ideals that had guided them into more general propositions of disciplinary well-being. Contrariwise, we presumed that there would be less consensus regarding meretricious matters within the field.

We were incorrect. Nearly 40% of the respondents came together to criticize the ideological developments that they saw unfolding in criminology, most notably (though not all were specific) the movement toward Marxist perspectives. "Ideology whether in theory or in method is pretentiously seen as 'new paradigms,' 'theories,' 'methods,' " said one respondent. Another regarded as unhealthy "the tendency on the part of many to reject unthinkingly the ideas and research of those with whom they disagree." "The substitution of ideology for social science" was what annoyed a third respondent. Two others deplored, in their words, "radical, wildly leftist, nonscientific voices," and "Marxist rhetoric and ideological narrowness." The feeling tone in regard to unhealthy developments was notably stronger than that used to convey information about perceived invigorating conditions.

It is obvious that, for whatever reasons, the highly-cited elders in criminology do not have a sense that all is perfectly well in their area of work. In so amorphous an enterprise as social science research, where there are no demonstrable end-products that fit consensual standards of worth, such as would be true of a cure for cancer, new paradigms are disconcerting. Social science ideas compete in a very free-floating marketplace where a constellation of elements—friendship, fad, opportunity, outlet, ability, novelty, timing, explanatory power, among many others—coalesce to determine what survives and flourishes and what becomes evanescent. One can gauge how fragile a process this is by the much greater proportion of submissions that generate disagreement from reviewers of professional papers in the social sciences as compared with the natural sciences (Cole and Cole, 1973). Such observations do not, however, undercut in any way (nor, for that matter, do they support) the validity of the perceived unhealthy elements in criminology as reported by our sample.

Recommendations to newcomers. The focus in the recommendations that were offered to newcomers in the field, almost all of which were communicated in one- to three-sentence responses, was heavily toward the importance of early training for later success. Two items stood out: first, secure a very strong background in theory, and especially in quantitative skills; and second, concentrate your energies on a particular subject and stay with that subject, developing a vested interest and producing a body of cumulative, interwoven research. Eclecticism clearly was not in favor; neither was theorizing, except as a consequence of the need for building a super-structure onto a solidly constructed foundation of field work.[5] Field experience was also strongly recommended as a means for acquiring firsthand information of the milieus and the persons about whom the criminologist would later write. A typical response in this vein, though much longer than its fellows, was:

> Through extensive training in sociological and social psychological theory generally to adopt a strong sociological approach to deviance and crime. To develop along with quantitative research methods a skill in qualitative research. To become personally familiar with the data of human experience, namely with deviants and criminal offenders themselves and not to depend upon secondary sources and punch cards gathered by others.

A more general platform was this:

> Read everything you can, have as much direct experience as you can, take as your goal a just and humane system of criminal law, and keep an open mind.

There were, in addition, four responses that stressed the need for historical training, both in criminology and in general subject areas, as essential for later sophisticated work. Only one respondent, however, noted that international or cross-cultural exposure would be a desideratum.

What have you learned? Our fifth question asked: "If you were to summarize things that you have learned during your professional life about scholarship and academic existence, what stands out most prominently?" Respondents could, of course, comment either on professional issues, such as scholarly matters, or on the kinds of personal pleasures or dissatisfactions that they might have experienced in their careers. We had anticipated that, given the phrase "professional life" in the forepart of the question, most responses would concentrate on intellectual issues. We also had thought that this question and the previous one—which sought advice from respondents for newcomers to the field—would produce largely similar responses. We were wrong on both counts.

The largest number of respondents with similar kinds of answers chose to tell us that academic life had been pleasant and rewarding. "The satisfaction of guiding young people in exciting ways of scholarship" was what one respondent noted. The most ebullient response in this genre took the following form:

> Those who participate in research and professional organizations have the most fun, make the best teachers, and are the more interesting to be around. Being a professor is the best job in the world.

Another response was in the same vein, and even more enthusiastic:

> It's a great life! Professors tend to be narrow minded, but decent in contrast to other people who tend to be narrow minded but not decent.

Beyond the expressions of personal contentment with their lot, several of the respondents addressed more scholarly kinds of issues. Here there were various stresses. One recurrent message focused on the need to buttress theoretical statements with a multitude of field investigations. Though the issue was stated in a variety of ways, the congruence of belief on the importance of this approach was striking.

At the same time, running through a goodly number of comments were sideswipes at colleagues, usually in the form of what might be taken for goodnatured passing jabs. "Sociologists need to be skeptics; too few are," noted one respondent as part of a longer answer. "There is too great a tendency to search for the exotica," another lamented. "Sociologists like to talk, but few wish to put what they say into print, which may be fortunate," was one rather acid reply. This respondent went on to stress the essential loneliness of scholarly work, a stress that pervades self-examination by fiction writers (see, e.g., Plimpton, 1963), though we found only this single expression from our cohort. A last respondent noted in passing the frustration occasionally engendered by administrators, funders, and "lazy colleagues," but he, too, came down finally on the rosy side after suggesting the foregoing thorns: "It's a hassle, but worth it."

The only comment that even mildly suggested that there might be concern in the group for the fact that contemporary work would render their contributions anachronistic was the quotation by one respondent, taken from (and credited to) Satchell Paige, the black baseball pitcher who, because of segregation, made it to the major leagues only after his career was on a downward path. What this scholar said he had learned was: "Keep moving and don't look back; something might be gaining on you."

Would you do it over again? This question affords an opportunity to operationalize a rather interesting idea: given that you have but one life to live, do you have such strong regrets about what you did with it that you now wish you had done otherwise?

We had not expected such a strong and enthusiastic endorsement of career choice from the group. One respondent thought that, given the chance, perhaps he would prefer to have done something in the theater, another in sculpture, while a third only regretted that he had shifted his interests between criminology and social statistics. Had the last respondent to do it over: "I would have attempted to become a master of some single subject rather than be a jack of several or more." Others interpreted the question in restrictive ways: they merely would have gotten better training, they said, noting particular gaps in their quantitative skills and in their knowledge of economics and law, in particular. The two more articulate responses siding with the heavy majority were these:

> I would enter no other field, or do anything different with my life. I regard criminology/deviance as lying at the substantive center of sociological concern, dealing as it does with issues of order-disorder, continuity-change, conflict-consensus, and (although neglected) justice-injustice.

> Despite some disadvantages (department organization, committees, teaching and other regulations, etc.) I feel I definitely would choose to be a professor for the freedom, the scholarly life, research opportunities, and the travel. I chose it because it was a professor who got "paid to read books." Deviance and criminology are the only fields in which I would be interested in sociology. Sometimes I feel I would have preferred to be an anthropologist which was my original interest, but which I could not continue because of a lack of teaching position.

CONCLUSION

The impetus for our attempt to gather together in this fashion some of the views of highly cited criminologists was our belief that there is a dearth of personal information available to younger academics about the career upon which they are embarking. It is much in the manner that young persons in the United States today tend to be cut off from whatever lessons about life they might absorb from their grandparents—even if the lesson is only that people can survive despite how bleak prospects might at one time have appeared. And that they can look backward with, if not pleasure, at least a sense of perspective and calm.

There exists little deep-probing biographical material on behavioral science scholars, and barely any of consequence on criminologists. In part, scholars tend to lead rather routine, even dreary, lives (but see contra Dorfman, 1934, on Thorstein Veblen) when examined in terms of popular appeal—and certainly when compared to many politicians, generals, and novelists. In part, this is because scholarly contributions are in the realm of ideas; in part it is because, particularly in more recent times, huge distances have existed between the exercise of power and the practice of social science in academic settings. The most far-ranging inquiry into the origins and ideas of criminologists (Snodgrass, 1972) required study of the lives and works of half a dozen persons to fill out a book-length manuscript.

The absence of personal materials, like the absence of more systematic training for teaching chores and for writing (in contrast to researching) leaves to word-of-mouth, conference hallways, folklore, and chance experiences the transmission of a broad range of information about a young scholar's chosen field of work. The interviews with well-known criminologists that were featured in *Issues in Criminology* (but are no longer conducted since that journal's incorporation with *Crime and Social Justice*) provided an important opportunity for the circulation of individual views about some aspects of the trade. We could learn from the persons interviewed how they went about their work, how they came to enter the field, where they thought it was going, and where they believed it ought to go. They might note the impact of book reviews on their efforts, the relative merit of writing articles against writing books, and their attitudes about teaching, research, and administrative posts. None of these may be profoundly important matters, but they tend to occupy (and understandably so) enormous amounts of time and emotional energy among practitioners in any social science fields, and they are deserving of more attention than they have received.

We would not want to pretend that the results of our cursory survey provide anything more than a mild flavor of responses to a few interesting questions. We found the replies generally informative and, at times, a bit surprising, particularly in regard to the pleasure with which the respondents look back upon their academic careers. One must remember, however, that our sample was composed of professionally successful scholars; how those of roughly the same age who had not done quite so well would have responded is another matter. Our respondents did not once mention financial matters, a subject often of consummate concern to their junior colleagues; nor did they, contrary to what others might think,[6] at any time note that they found the academic life stifling or monastic. Nor did they press their own claims to preeminence in either direct or subtle ways.

Criminology's successful elders, if those who responded to our inquiry represent a fair sample, wish they had been better trained, particularly in law and economics, and they seem to deplore their failure to concentrate exclusively on a particular segment of the discipline.[7] But, all in all, as they (and perhaps only they) see things, work in criminology, except for recent Marxist incursions, seems to them to have had an agreeable past, and they appear to be able to look forward to a promising future.

NOTES

1. The most dramatic enactment of this condition was performed by a colleague of one of the present authors. If he received a book in the mail, he immediately would open it to the index to determine if his name was included. If it was not, he would angrily throw the book into the mailroom trash basket. Fortunately, he was an extremely prominent scholar, so that only rarely was he obliged to discard arriving volumes. His response was totally honest, and may provide an important insight into why he was renowned in his field.

2. We want to thank Marvin E. Wolfgang, Robert Figlio, and Terence Thornberry for sharing with us the data from which this sample was drawn.

3. In alphabetical order, the most-cited scholars are: David Abrahamsen, Ronald Akers, Harry Anslinger, Vilhelm Aubert, David Ausubel, Sidney Axelrad, Milton Barron, Howard S. Becker, Albert Biderman, Herbert Bloch, David Bordua, Mary Cameron, Isidor Chein, Roland Chilton, John Clark, Marshall Clinard, Richard Cloward, Albert Cohen, Donald Cressey, Robert Dentler, Kurt Eissler, Kai Erikson, Harold Finestone, Paul Gebhard, Sheldon Glueck, Erving Goffman, Martin Gold, Manfred Guttmacher, Starke Hathaway, Andrew Henry, Travis Hirschi, John Kitsuse, Malcolm Klein, Solomon Kobrin, William Kvaraceus, Bernard Lander, Edwin Lemert, Alfred Lindesmith, David Matza, William McCord, Maud Merrill, Robert Merton, Walter Miller, Elio Monachesi, Fred Murphy, Ivan Nye, Lloyd Ohlin, David Pittman, Austin Porterfield, Otto Pollak, Herbert Quay, Walter Reckless, Fritz Redl, Albert Reiss, Joseph Roucek, Calvin Schmid, Karl Schuessler, Thorsten Sellin, William Sheldon, James Short, Jerome Skolnick, Charles Snyder, Irving Spergel, Edwin H. Sutherland, Gresham Sykes, Paul Tappan, George Vold, William Wattenberg, Frederic Wertham, Marvin Wolfgang, and Lewis Yablonsky.

4. And *him* it always was, except for two persons: Mary Owen Cameron and Maud Merrill.

5. Note Scott's (1971: 3) observation: "Sociologists with reputations as theorists are more likely to study the writing of earlier theorists than contemporary research literature."

6. See, for example, the comment of Supreme Court Justice Oliver Wendell Holmes:

[A]cademic life is but half life—it was withdrawal from the fight in order to utter smart things that cost you nothing except the thinking them from a cloister. My wife thinks I unconsciously began to grow sober with an inarticulate sense of limitation in the few months of my stay in Cambridge. . . .

Business in the world is unhappy, often seems mean, and always challenges your power to idealize the brute fact—but it hardens the fiber and I think is more likely to make more of a man of one who turns it to success. . . . [T]he line of *most* resistance is the one to choose [Howe, 1963: 282].

7. Justice Holmes again:

It is interesting to understand how men come to prefer a professional to a general reputation—and for the former, which hardly outlives the greatest . . . will sacrifice every hope of the other [Howe, 1957: 195].

REFERENCES

BECKER, H. P. (1950) Through Values to Social Interpretation. Durham, NC: Duke Univ. Press.
COLE, J. and S. COLE (1973) Social Stratification in Science. Chicago: Univ. of Chicago Press.
DORFMAN, J. (1934) Thorstein Veblen and His America. New York: Viking.

HOWE, M. D. (1963) Justice Oliver Wendell Holmes: The Proving Years, 1870-1881. Cambridge, MA: Harvard Univ. Press.

——— (1963) Justice Oliver Wendell Holmes: The Shaping Years, 1841-1870. Cambridge, MA: Harvard Univ. Press.

MERTON, R. K. (1957) "Priorities in scientific discovery." Amer. Soc. Rev. 22: 635-659.

PLIMPTON, G. (1963) Writers at Work. New York: Viking.

RIESMAN, D. (1957) "Law and sociology: notes on recruitment, training, and colleagueship." Stanford Law Rev. 9: 643-673.

SCOTT, J. F. (1971) Internalization of Norms. Englewood Cliffs, NJ: Prentice-Hall.

SELLIN, T. (1938) Culture Conflict and Crime. New York: Social Science Research Council.

SNODGRASS, J. (1972) "The American criminological tradition: portraits of men and ideology in a discipline." Unpublished Ph.D. dissertation, University of Pennsylvania.

ABOUT THE AUTHORS

Harry E. Allen is Professor, Administration of Justice, San Jose State University, and has served as Executive Counselor and Treasurer (1974-1978) of the American Society of Criminology and 1977 recipient of its Herbert Bloch Award. He has written numerous articles, monographs, and texts, including Corrections in America. *He is interested in corrections, criminal justice administration, and deviance. He will be vice-president of the American Society of Criminology for 1980.*

Marshall B. Clinard is Professor of Sociology at the University of Wisconsin— Madison. He is author of a number of books, including Sociology of Deviant Behavior, *and coauthor of* Crime in Developing Countries *and* Criminal Behavior Systems: A Typology. *His latest book,* Cities with Little Crime: The Case of Switzerland, *is in press. He received the Edwin H. Sutherland award in 1971 and was named a Fellow of the American Society of Criminology in 1977.*

Donald R. Cressey has conducted research in five different prisons, in a police department, in a probation-parole agency, in a prosecuting attorney's office, and in several juvenile courts. He has published ten books, ranging in subject matter from embezzlement and organized crime to plea bargaining. One of his books, Principles of Criminology *(with the late Edwin H. Sutherland, 1883-1950), is now in its tenth edition (1978). Professor Cressey has been Visiting Professor at the University of Cambridge, Hebrew University, Oslo University, and the Australian National University. He was the 1967 recipient of the Sutherland Award of the American Society of Criminology, and his research also has been honored by the Illinois Academy of Criminology, Indiana University, Iowa State University, and the University of California, Santa Barbara.*

Simon Dinitz is Professor of Sociology at Ohio State University and Senior Fellow at the Academy for Contemporary Problems. He is a former president of the American Society of Criminology, former editor of its journal, and a recipient of the Society's Edwin Sutherland Award.

John Dombrink, a graduate of the University of San Francisco, is a graduate student in sociology at the University of California, Berkeley, and a research assistant at the Center for the Study of Law and Society.

Gilbert Geis is a Professor in the Program in Social Ecology, University of California, Irvine. He is past president of the American Society of Criminology, and is coeditor (with Robert F. Meier) of White-Collar Crime: Offenses in Business, Politics and the Professions *(Free Press, 1977). His research interests include white-collar crime, forcible rape, and victimology.*

Daniel Glaser is Professor of Sociology at the University of Southern California, and author of numerous articles on criminology and drug addiction. His most recent book is Crime in Our Changing Society *(Holt, Rinehart and Winston, 1978), and he edited the* Handbook of Criminology *(Rand McNally, 1974). Glaser is a former Chairman of the Criminology Section of the American Sociological Association and is currently Chairman of the Crime and Juvenile Delinquency Division of the Society for the Study of Social Problems. In 1976 he received the Sutherland Award of the American Society of Criminology.*

C. R. Jeffery, Professor of Criminology at Florida State University and 1978 president of the American Society of Criminology, was recipient of the Edwin Sutherland Award of the Society, and has received a Fulbright-Hays award for The Netherlands for 1978-1979. He is author of numerous works, including Crime Prevention Through Environmental Design, *and is a former editor of* Criminology: An Interdisciplinary Journal.

Andrew Karmen is Assistant Professor of Sociology at John Jay College of Criminal Justice. He has taught at Boston State College, University of Lowell, and City College of New York. He is author of articles on heroin addiction, police practices, and other social problems.

Donal E. J. MacNamara, Professor of Criminology and Corrections, John Jay College of Criminal Justice, City University of New York, is a past president of the American Society of Criminology and co-editor with Edward Sagarin of Criminology: An Interdisciplinary Journal.

Robert F. Meier is affiliated with the Department of Sociology, Washington State University. He is coeditor (with Gilbert Geis) of White-Collar Crime: Offenses in Business, Politics and the Professions *(Free Press, 1977). His research interests include processes of deviance and social control, and the sociology of law.*

Charles L. Newman is Professor and Director of the Center for Criminal Justice Research and Planning of the Institute of Urban Studies, University of Texas at Arlington. He is former president of the American Society of Criminology and former editor of Criminology: An Interdisciplinary Journal; *is Professor Emeritus of Pennsylvania State University; and among his other work has authored a comprehensive study of American jails.*

Walter C. Reckless is Professor Emeritus of Sociology at the Ohio State University and served three years (1964-1966) as President of the American Society of Criminology. An Edwin Sutherland Award recipient (1963), he has authored numerous major articles, theories, and texts, including the classic The Crime Problem.

Edward Sagarin is Professor of Sociology at City College and City University of New York. He is a former president of the American Society of Criminology and coeditor with Donal E.J. MacNamara of Criminology: An Interdisciplinary Journal. *He is editor of* Deviance and Social Change *(a Sage publication in an annual series), coauthor with MacNamara of* Sex, Crime, and the Law, *and author and editor of numerous works on crime, deviance, sexual behavior, and related subjects.*

Jerome H. Skolnick is Director of the Center for the Study of Law and Society and Professor of Law (Jurisprudence and Social Policy) at the University of California, Berkeley. In 1972 he was given the American Society of Criminology's August Vollmer Award "for distinguished research in Criminal Justice and Law Enforcement."

Marvin E. Wolfgang is Professor of Sociology at the University of Pennsylvania and director of the Center for Studies in Criminology and Criminal Law at that institution. He is a former president of the American Society of Criminology and winner of its August Vollmer Award. Among his many publications are Patterns in Criminal Homicide *and* The Subculture of Violence, *the latter co-authored with Franco Ferracuti.*

Peter C. Yeager is a graduate of the University of Minnesota, and received his M.S. at the University of Wisconsin—Madison, where he is now completing his dissertation. He is Senior Research Assistant on a research project on corporate crime for which Clinard is Project Director.